SONG OF RITA JOE

SONG OF RITA JOE
AUTOBIOGRAPHY OF A MI'KMAQ POET

RITA JOE

with the assistance of
Lynn Henry

RAGWEED
THE ISLAND PUBLISHER

Ragweed Press acknowledges the generous support of The Canada Council and the Department of Canadian Heritage, Multiculturalism. Ragweed Press would like to thank the Institute for the Study of Women, Mount Saint Vincent University, for kind permission to use "The Honour Song of the Micmac," by Rita Joe, in the preparation of this manuscript. "The Honour Song of the Micmac" was originally published in *Kelusultiek: Original Women's Voices of Atlantic Canada* (Institute for the Study of Women, Mount Saint Vincent University, 1994). We would also like to thank Professor Gordon E. Smith, of Queen's University, for his kind assistance and generous cooperation, and for permission to publish his musical transcriptions of Rita Joe's songs. Some of the poems in this book were first published in *Poems of Rita Joe* (Abanaki Press, 1978), *Song of Eskasoni: More Poems of Rita Joe* (Ragweed Press, 1988) and *Lnu and Indians We're Called* (Ragweed Press, 1991).

Cover and section art: Rock Drawings of the Micmac by Teresa Marshall
Cover photograph: Carol Kennedy
Printed and bound in Canada by: Hignell Printing Ltd.

Published by:
Ragweed Press
P.O. Box 2023
Charlottetown, PEI
C1A 7N7

Canadian Cataloguing in Publication Data

Joe, Rita, 1932-

Song of Rita Joe

ISBN 0-921556-59-4

1. Joe, Rita, 1932- . 2. Poets, Canadian — 20th century — Biography. 3. Indian women — Canada — Biography. I. Title.

PS8569.O265Z53 1996   C811'.54   C96-950005-X
PR9199.3.J63Z46 1996

I dedicate this book to my children and
their children's children, and to all people
who read about and identify with my life.
Alasutmay ujit kilow *(I pray for you).*

ACKNOWLEDGMENTS

I would like to thank Ragweed Press, the people at the Band Office in Eskasoni, and all the people who have helped me to prepare this book. I especially thank Lynn Henry, for her skills, patience and dedication.

CONTENTS

INTRODUCTION

One morning when I was just a young Curatorial Assistant at the Nova Scotia Museum, Sarah Denny of the Micmac Association for Cultural Studies came into my office, bringing her friend Rita Joe. They were like two great queens paying a visit of state. We went into the storage areas of the Museum to look at shell beads. Rita wanted to recreate some of the Mi'kmaq wampum belts. I recall she had the quietest way of speaking — she made about as much noise as an ant's foot. Who would have thought that this woman, who looked as if she had been made out of rose petals, could manifest such a powerful voice?

Over the following twenty years, I was to learn so much from Rita Joe and from Sarah Denny, but I had a particular bond with Rita because we both loved words. We loved to write and we enjoyed talking about our writing to each other. Sometimes Rita would read me poems over the phone; sometimes I would send her something I'd written and ask for her comments. She has reviewed my books and given me permission to use portions of her poems to illuminate my own essays. I remember when she showed me the first pages of this work. She told me stories while I read her words, and I cried over many of them.

Rita Joe has had a harsh life — orphaned at age five, growing up in a series of bleak foster homes, surviving the years at residential school and a difficult marriage — but she constantly works with her past through her writing. It is a very brave thing to write about one's own life. Painful memories, deeply buried, blocked, boarded over, still overshadow us — "… like a bird of prey," notes Rita, "until it is written." In her prose and in her poetry, Rita Joe shows us that we are not alone. We can come to wholeness and, like her, we can bring compassion into the context of our lives.

Rita also has a mission: to sensitize everyone to the pain caused by racism and by insensitivity to, and ignorance of, other cultures. It is the pain felt daily by all First Nations people when they deal with the outside world. Rita has worked tirelessly to eliminate biased histories and school texts, which often depicted First Nations peoples in derogatory ways, using nouns such as "savages." First Nations triumphs in war, for example, were referred to as "massacres," where European triumphs were "victories." Perjorative terms such as "squaw" or "brave" or "buck" were substituted for "women" and "men." And First Nations were — and often still are — treated as if they are all the same. They have been reduced to cheap Hollywood-movie common denominators. In her poetry and in her lectures to audiences of all ages, Rita has done more to bridge the gap between her culture and mine than almost anyone else I know.

Another way in which she has contributed to such understanding is through her encouragement of other Native writers. Now, in 1996, there are a number of First Nations writers and poets in this area, telling the other side of our mutual history: Katharine Sorbey, Helen Sylliboy, Shirley Mitchell, Shirley Kiju Kawi, Phyllis Paul, Kim Brooks, Cathy Martin, Bernadette Martin and Dixie Wheeler. Their numbers include excellent poets such as Shirley Bear and Mary Louise Martin; historians and essayists such as Andrea Bear Nicholas; storytellers like Raymond Clermont; and researchers and linguists such as Bernie Francis. Rita Joe was one of the first writers to blaze this spirit road across the stars for Native writers.

Now, reading this final draft of Rita's autobiography, memories flood back. I realize that the greatest gift she ever gave me is one I learned from watching her reach out in loving communication to everyone around her. She taught me through her compassion, her ability to forgive, and her great kindness to non-Mi'kmaq persons. Her words — her powerful voice — remind me of this gift, and I feel once again how honoured I am to know Rita Joe.

— *Ruth Holmes Whitehead*
The Nova Scotia Museum
February 1996

THE OLD WOMAN DANCE

PROLOGUE

I am an old woman now.

When I dance the powwow, I cannot dance it like the young ones do, because I limp on my left side. But I do dance. It's called an old woman dance: dragging your feet around on the ground, just moving.

I enter the multi-purpose building
Where the powwow is held
And stand amidst the crowd
Hoping to see someone familiar, to say hello.

The drummers begin to play, singing songs
That touch my heart.
A man comes out of the crowd,
And dances by me.
I am curious. "Who is he," I ask.
A medicine man from out of the province, I am told.

I join the dance, sometimes closing my eyes,
Dancing the elderly woman dance,
My feet flat, close to earth.
The song takes a long time to end
And we dance.
When we walk away from the floor
My feet are light, I walk on air
And I feel fear.

I explain the feeling to the medicine man.
"You have been in a ceremonial healing dance,"
He says. "Sit out the next one."
So I sit, amazement in my heart,
Ready to tell about the elderly woman dance.

When I dance in a powwow, I follow my heart. My heart is what has moved me all along. Nothing but your own heart has answers to the questions you ask.

It is hard to follow the white man's way. We Native people must use our own way, use what our own hearts tell us, no matter what we talk about — welfare, housing, problems in marriage, spirituality. Throughout my life, I have tried to remember what my elders told me. I remember the things my dad told me when I was a child; even during my years at the Shubenacadie Indian Residential School, when I got mixed up and flustered about the spiritual part of things, I tried to remember. When I was in my thirties, I began to write down what I remembered.

My greatest wish is that there will be more writing from my people, and that our children will read it. I have said again and again that our history would be different if it had been expressed by us. My people were known as great orators, and the ones I have heard and read about have presented their views truthfully, but the way our views were passed into history and literature by the so-called "discoverers" has done harm in more ways than can be imagined.

I hope the future holds a better promise. Our heritage has not died. It lives in the eyes of our people. Those eyes are sometimes sad, sometimes hostile, sometimes hidden, sometimes curious, watching to see what you will do next. I, too, have been a watcher. I have watched this world that we live in since my childhood; I have watched it from the rooted world of my mom, dad, foster homes and Indian Residential School. Some people would say that this world was bad. I know people who came from this world and have gone on to productive lives, and I know some who have not, their scars too deep. My message is gentle: If one wishes to be healed, one must dwell on the positive.

Today, it is the image of my people that is uppermost in my mind. It is our beauty that must be discovered now — and this thought inspires the next: *Nenwite'ten ke'luk weji tu'ap* (Remember: I found the good). *Jika'winen we'jitutqsip kutoy ninen* (Look at us and you, too, will find the good).

Being strangers in our own land is a sad story, but, if we can speak, we may turn this story around. That is why I write today: Let us have our say, or none at all. *'Iknmulek na! (We give! Let us give!)*

SONG OF MY GIRLHOOD
(1932 — 1950)

EPITEJIJ

The winding old road is all that remains
The church and grounds
Where my forefathers lay
Whycocomagh, *We'kopa'q*
The end of water,
and I, Rita Joe, am one of the children.

I was born in Whycocomagh, Cape Breton, in the eastern part of Canada, on March 15, 1932. My parents, Joseph (Josie) Gould Bernard and Annie (Googoo) Bernard had seven children. Sonwel, a boy, had died earlier in infancy, and the seventh would die with my mother in 1937, when I was five. I was the sixth, and the youngest surviving child. My three brothers, Charlie (whom we called Soln), Roddy and Matt, were eleven, eight and four years older than me, and my sister Annabel was five years older. From two earlier marriages of my father's there were also Susie, a much older sister, and William, who was thirty-five when I was born.

As far back as I can remember, I had a loving family. We were very poor, but I try to remember the positive things. I cannot remember my family being loud or angry. Everybody was soft-spoken and gentle, even though we had such a sad lot. We were poor and the neighbours were poor and everybody did the best they could to help their neighbours. The contact among people was gentle and loving. That's the part I remember.

My father was born in 1864 or 1865. When he was in his twenties, he changed his name from Josie Gould to Josie Bernard. There are many stories about why he did this. It could be that he did not want to be named after a woman — my great-grandmother Mary Ann Gould. Her father had been a sailor who briefly left his ship to be with my great-great grandmother Gould. The sailor's name is not known, but the child who was born a while later — my great-grandmother — had light features. I heard that the man acknowledged his baby in a letter and the letter was taken to court to prove that he was the father, but the people who were asked to swear on the bible about the truth of this claim could not be sure. Still, right down to this day, there are a lot of blue and hazel eyes in my family. Sometimes I wonder about that; in my heart, I care about where I come from. The Native part of me I am sure of; I honour it whole, and respect all other cultures. *Kisulkw* (the Great Spirit) looks after the rest.

> In the early years, my dad's name was Josie Gould
> Sometime later he changed his name to Bernard.
> When I was born the changed name was mine
> Today I correct from afar.
>
> The reason he gave was: not from a woman
> He wanted to be known, his name,
> But from a man's man his ego travelled.
> I am his daughter, humility is my fame.
>
> In the early years, my dad was Josie Gould
> The Mi'kmaq never let him forget it.
> Today I say what is true:
> To the name Gould I have a right.

My dad was a commanding figure, tall in stature, with a ruddy complexion, white hair parted on the side and a lopsided grin. I have his picture, so I know he was a handsome man. I remember him being strict but kind, soft-spoken but persuasive. Sometimes, when I listen to myself speak, I can hear how my speech is like his. My father was in his fifties or sixties when he married my mother, and she was only sixteen. She was his third wife. When she died, I remember my dad looking around again. So you can imagine how romantic he was, outliving three wives and still looking for another.

My mother, Annie, was the only daughter of Isobel and Francis Googoo. She was a loving person; her loving arms are not easily forgotten. When I try to visualize my times with her, I remember them like hazy motion pictures of years gone by. I can see her laughing with her very white teeth, her bosom my cushion as I lay my head there. I remember her being soft, so I think she might have been fat. Soln used to tell me he would pick spruce gum for mother because she liked chewing it and it made her teeth white. She would chew it until it turned pink. When I was growing up, people would tell me, "Annie liked chewing spruce gum — even snapping it in church!" I think she must have liked singing, too, because I was told that when she died and people waked her, they heard the strains of a song in the air: *"Mouiemto'q a'la'nej* (O come let us adore him)." And I remember she used to laugh a lot and tease me. Her attitude was that of a young person.

In Whycocomagh I lived with my parents and my brother Soln, the oldest of my mother's five children. He was always looking out for us younger ones; he was the good son whom our dad favoured and our mom adored. I loved each of my brothers, but there was something special about Soln. I thought of him as the older brother I could depend on no matter what — the one who could always solve any problem.

My other brothers, Matt and Roddy, were away at the Shubenacadie Indian Residential School. People in Whycocomagh called Matt *"Moqnja'tu'wi',"* meaning "putting the sugar on things." He was also called "Misekn (Rags)" at the Shubenacadie school. I remember I called him that once, and he laughed. He was closest to Roddy because they grew up together at the school. Roddy, I remember, was a happy-go-lucky little guy.

My sister Annabel was living with my grandparents in Whycocomagh. She had been with them since the age of three, and Roddy had also lived with them for a time before going to the residential school. I remember Grandma took good care of Annabel, who was very pretty and had long braided hair. I was skinny, with constantly sore eyes — the ugly duckling in the family.

■ ■ ■

My father is working on pieces of wood. He dips them in hot water, carefully bending them, at times carving something on them with a drawknife (a very sharp knife with two handles, one on either side). The *tesipojij* (workhorse bench) he uses is like a little horse. It has footpedals that are used like a vice so that the hands are free to work.

I am always nearby while my father works because I like playing with the very white shavings from the wood. I am told to put them into a woodbox near the stove. The job is important to me because I like doing things for my father. He is cross sometimes, but mellow most of the time.

Suddenly, I hear *Kiju'* (Mother) and my father argue. My mother is weeping as she sits on the floor beside me. I encircle her neck with my arms. "Don't be mean to Kiju'," I say. My father smiles and my mother is softly laughing.

When I was small
I used to help my father
Make axe handles.
Coming home from the wood with a bundle
Of *maskwi, snawey, aqamoq,*
My father would chip away,
Carving with a crooked knife,
Until a well-made handle appeared,
Ready to be sandpapered
By my brother.

When it was finished
We started another,
Sometimes working through the night
With me holding a lighted shaving
To light their way
When our kerosene lamp ran dry.

Then in the morning
My mother would be happy
That there would be food today
When my father sold our work.

■ ■ ■

The memory of my mother's passing is like something precious taken from you when you are happiest. The words I heard that day are like an echo in my mind.

"You must take Rita to *Kijinu* (Grandmother)," my dad told Soln. I wondered why I had to go so early in the morning; I wanted to be with my mom.

Soln pulled me to Grandma's in the box of my little wagon. When we arrived at her house, she looked so cross! "Annabel, take Rita to school with you," she said to my older sister. It must have been hard on my grandma, worrying about my mother and having a five-year-old underfoot.

I was glad to go to school; I had never been there before and I was happy being part of a class. "This is a dog. This is a cat," I recited, along with the other children. Then came a ring, and a pause. Another ring; pause. We all looked at each other. We knew what this meant: Somebody in the community had died. Our teacher, Mr. MacDonald, also knowing the meaning of the church bell angelus, let out an early recess. I think he told us to go home.

I remember coming out of the school and right at the corner of the road — Reservation Road; the school is still in the same place today — I saw my dad hanging onto a fence post, not moving, just standing there. "What's wrong, Dad?" Annabel and I both asked at the same time, in Mi'kmaq. "What's the matter?" He had the saddest eyes I ever saw; the look in them is still with me today.

He told us, "Go to your grandma. Go to your grandma's house." I guess he knew his wife was dying. He made sure that they got the doctor from downtown. I remember the doctor rode in a wagon pulled by one horse.

We ran over to my grandmother's house, which was near the school. My *kujinu* (grandfather) was already there. He had been working out on the water beside Whycocomagh, when someone said to him, *"Na'taqma'si* (Go ashore)." So he went ashore and walked slowly towards the house, where he sat on the steps, a sad look on his face. He knew that something bad was coming.

My grandmother was standing at the door of the house. When Annabel and I reached her, she said to my grandfather, *"Pla'n* (Francis), there must be something going on." She was agitated, still not knowing what had happened, but sensing something bad as well. Finally, she saw the chief, Gabriel Silliboy, coming down the road. "What's going on, Gabriel?" I heard her holler.

"Annie is gone. Annie is dead."

I wondered, Who is Annie?

I turned and saw my grandfather crying. It is hard to see a man cry, especially a grandfather.

Grandma fell backwards onto the floor. I remember watching Annabel put a wet cloth on her face, trying to wake her up. They held each other, crying, while I looked on, terrified, wondering what was happening. Finally, Grandma got up. She pointed a finger at me. Sixty years later, I still see that pointy finger. "*Ki'l ktla taqn*! (It is your fault!)" she said.

I did not want to be the cause of my mother's death, and, throughout my life, Grandma's words haunted me. I kept thinking that, maybe, when I slept with my mother, I kicked her in the stomach. Once I had my own children, I knew that a small child does not kick that hard and I did not feel so bad anymore. I did not know what else I could have done to cause her death, but I kept on asking questions about it. Many years later, I questioned the midwife, Mrs. Jessie Jeddore, who had attended my mother at the time of her death. She said, "I think your mother died with the child inside her as a result of the cold from fishing for smelts." My mother, nine months pregnant, used to go out on the ice and sit on a box with fir branches under her feet and fish. The way the midwife explained it, the cold might have got into my mother's body this way, and the baby could not be born. I told the midwife about my grandmother's pointy finger, and she said, "I don't remember you being a difficult birth or anything. I attended your mother when you were born and you were normal. There was nothing. Don't listen to your grandmother. She was a cross old lady anyway. It didn't mean anything." So I finally put this out of my mind.

When I was taken back to my house later the day my mother died, there were many people there. I looked around and saw a lot of food: cakes, pies and goodies. I was led to a table and given food. Then my father took me by the hand and lifted me up to see my mother. She was in a long box. "She's cold, Dad," I said.

He turned his face to the wall.

The year 1937
My world comes tumbling down.
In childbirth my mother dies,
The baby goes with her.
"It was from the cold ice," they say,
Her fishing for smelts to feed the family.
Why her?
There were other people fishing.
Why her?
I shout even today.

■ ■ ■

When a Mi'kmaq person dies, immediate supplications for the dead are recited by the nearest relative. Then a three-day wake is held, at which Native prayers and hymns are sung, and food and comfort are given freely.

The Mass for the Dead is sung by the priest, and we answer with prayers in Mi'kmaq. The hymns we hear in our own tongue often move us to tears, for they are more beautiful to us in our own language.

When the body is lowered into the ground, Native choir members sing a hymn that has been handed down for centuries.

Ma'lta elasnl Se'susil
Saqamaw, wula I'mu'sipn,
Mu pa npisoqq wijikitiekaq,
Skatu kejitu nike',
Kisu'lk iknimultal msit ta'n tel-tamjil.

(Martha said to Jesus:
Lord, if you had been here
My brother would not have died,
But I know that even now
God will give you whatever you ask of him.)

■ ■ ■

After my mother's funeral, Roddy and Matt stayed in residential school and my father, Soln and I went to my grandmother's house to live. My grandmother seemed very angry and yelled at my father. At that time, my dad depended on Annabel too much. She did all the cooking, washing, sewing and other chores for my father, and the responsibility fell on her to care for me. She couldn't do it. She was ten or eleven years old and searching for something, too. Finally, Dad left Soln with my grandparents and took Annabel and me away from there. I went into a succession of foster homes. "*Sitnaqn na* (She is an orphan)." I heard those words often from the age of five until I was twelve.

> I believe in fate, no alternative.
> All the reasons we are who we are.
> Me a foster child in so many homes
> Being cared for by people as poor as I am.
> We survive.
>
> The year 1937
> I saw moderation in bits or pieces.
> The pictures like shadows, a veil at times.
> Like a puzzle, the pages turn slowly.
> The scar is there like a bird of prey,
> Until it is written.
>
> Don't turn the page, the hurt will be there again.
> But I have to tell, this is life:
> I am gone, the word is all that is left.

There are many stories from each foster home. The homes were in nearby Mi'kmaq communities, where the people knew my dad. I would stay for six months, maybe three months, maybe a year, two months, a month, two weeks. There were so many different homes. Each time I was told that there was a new one, I would wonder: Where will I be going? What will the mama and papa be like? What will the children be like?

Mostly, I try to recall the good stories. Natives believe that if you are kind to *sitnaqn* (orphans), goodness will be returned to you. There were a lot of good houses in the different Native communities where I lived, and a lot of good mothers; I always remember the mothers. Native women everywhere are loving towards children. They would try to give me what I call indifferent love: no touching, except on the head. I remember one woman who lived down the street on one reservation. She would cut up old socks to make new, warm ones for me. And when I was on my way back from school, she would call me into her house to warm up and have something to eat. She was very kind to me.

I loved each of my mothers in each different home, and worked hard at being a good girl and being accepted. But the places I liked never lasted for long — pretty soon, I would be placed in another home. In all of the homes I was fed and given a good bed — a mattress on the floor or whatever the people could spare. The families took care of me and helped me to survive, but they did not give me loving parents. I would envy the children who had a real mother and father; I had real envy. I would stand there, watching the parents with their children, and whatever morsel of praise or love they gave me, I would accept. I learned very early in life that humility is how to earn your way into the heart of the person who's looking after you. I had to work hard for that affection — very hard.

Because of this experience, I consider myself to be a survivor. I have been a survivor since I was five years old. If I was hungry, I'd try to figure out a way to fill my stomach. I knew that my people were kind and compassionate, so I would go into any house on the reserve and stand by the door. I would fidget from the left foot to the right foot, until the lady of the house finally said, "Here's some bread, Rita. Load butter and jam on it, and go over there and eat it. Drink some milk, too." All the while I would say, "Thank you, thank you." And if I was hungry later, I would go to another house and do the same thing again. I knew all the shortcuts to survive.

Being a survivor means that you don't go crazy or blow your top. At times, it was very hard to survive. The experiences of my childhood, I'm reliving them yet — and I won't stop reliving them until I die.

■ ■ ■

My first foster home was in Membertou Reservation near Sydney. This was where my stepsister, Susie Marshall, lived. She was glad to see me and promised my father to take good care of me. I was given lots of pretty dresses and patent leather shoes and I took a bath in the washtub every day. Susie would dress me each morning and then go to work; women on the reserve took care of me while she was gone. Native communities are like extended family — everybody looks out for everybody else's kids — so there were a lot of people watching out for me. If I was on the road and in danger, I'd be scolded and told, "You stay over there in the yard; you're supposed to stay over there. Don't go away from there!" It was good for me to be on the reservation with my own people and to speak Mi'kmaq, which was the only language I knew then.

I spent much of my time across the road, playing with my cousin Wallace Bernard, who was about a year younger than I. Wallace and I got into a lot of mischief and, by the end of the day when I would see my sister coming down the road and run to meet her, I would be a mess. I remember one incident when Wallace's uncle, *A'wi* (Louis), held a bag of candy out to us and told us: "The one *mejukat* (who defecates) the fastest will get the candy!" I recall the candy looked good, but I knew Susie had a strong hand. I don't remember if Wallace took the dare. Today, I think *A'wi* must have teased us just to see what we would do.

I liked being Susie's *wkwejij* (sister), but her husband was mean. When he hit me, I would land across the room. I remember my dad visiting me once and bringing me a little bag of candy. That little bag of candy was my treasure. I carried it around with me after my dad left and never ate it. My brother-in-law noticed the little bag and took it away from me. I can still see the lifted stove cover and the little bag dropping into the fire. The tears that fell from me at that moment summed up the rejection I had felt since my mother had died. I cried for her to return, but she never did come back.

To be content with what we have
Comes to be the value of what we love.

To be the daughter of Josie Gould and Annie
Their winded path, I pass alone,
My brothers gone.
And love comes across the void.
Seeing the gentle trail in dream
I try to follow by clue:
E'e, kesalipni'k na — yes, they loved me.

■ ■ ■

Soon after this, Dad came and took me to a new foster home in Pictou Landing. I don't remember why he did this — perhaps he had made an arrangement with Mary, the woman I stayed with in Pictou Landing; I learned later that Mary was a cousin. I don't know what my dad was doing during this time; I think he must have been working in Millbrook, trying to earn his own way. I imagine he communicated by letter with the people in the foster homes, and if something happened or they got tired of looking after me they would write to my father and say, "Take Rita away."

I remember my new foster mother was kind and my new home was beautiful. One thing that sticks out in my memory is that the kitchen had wood walls — knotted pine — with wallpaper near the top. The husband made axe handles on his workhorse and the son was older than I and nice enough, although he ignored me most of the time. I was a nuisance to him; he was fourteen and I was only six.

One night, my foster mother and I were sitting on the floor watching her husband whittle an axe handle. We heard a door open in the other room — it was the son coming home. The husband put the axe handle down, went into the other room and closed the door. Later, I heard the sound of a severe beating. From that time on, I feared I would get a beating if I did not behave exactly as my foster parents wanted. I tried to do what I was told, no matter how unusual I thought the request. I still wonder why the son received those severe beatings.

I lived in that home for many months, and that's when I first went to school. I remember spying on a classroom with another girl; we were peeking in the windows, wondering what the children inside were doing. Finally, the teacher told us to come in and sit down, and very soon we were given crochet needles and shown how to crochet a tam. I don't know how long it took me to learn to crochet (and I don't remember learning my ABCs) but I remember this tam. When it was finished, I took the tam home and showed it to my foster mother, and, oh, she was so appreciative.

I also remember going to a particular house in this community and being taught Indian prayers by an old man. He had one leg that was bent, and he walked on crutches. All of us kids would go down to that old man's home and learn Native prayers. I often wonder: If I had stayed in Pictou Landing, would I know more Indian prayers today?

> I lament forgotten skills,
> While my deeds come from a new image.
> Companion wind bewails over the hills
> That fall from our customs and heritage.
>
> Regret stays with me.
> I reflect upon myself, unforgiving;
> Uncertainty returns to haunt
> The native ways I abandoned.
>
> The years barely leave a trace
> But the sun's warmth reminds my senses
> Not to yield completely.

One day, without warning, my dad came and placed me in another home. Many years later, when I visited Pictou Landing with my husband, I asked Mary, who had been my foster mother, "Why was I taken away? I appeared to be happy in that place, and you took good care of me."

She replied, "Well, there was a bog in the back — a swamp or a bog — and it was soft. And we lost you one day, we just lost you. We never knew where you were. All day you were missing." She told me that people went into the woods looking for me. When they found me, I was up to my armpits in the bog. I couldn't get out and I was worn out from crying for help. Of course, the community made a lot of noise about this and said Mary was not taking care of me properly. Someone got in touch with my dad and said I shouldn't live at that place, and I was taken out. But me, I liked that place.

I don't remember what discussions took place, but it always happened like that: All of a sudden, my father would pick me up and I would be in another home.

> At age seven
> To Springhill Junction we came,
> My father and I
> And sister Annabel.
>
> There we made our home
> Of birchbark and pole
> And a bed of pine branches.
> I remember its comfort.
>
> This was my home.
> A memory stands out —
> A wigwam high on the hill
> In nineteen thirty-eight.

■ ■ ■

The next place I went to was in Millbrook Reservation. There were a man and a woman and several boys, all much bigger than I was. That was a strange place altogether, and I was not related to the family, so I was very good. When you live in a foster home, you have to be good: You don't do anything wrong and you don't give anyone an excuse to scold you or beat you or whatever. When I was still very little I learned to be a good girl, to always help.

One boy in this home was the same age as me. Because I was an outsider, he and the other children would pinch me and pull my hair and take my food. Looking back on it today, I can see that they were little brats.

> I am happy
> The King and Queen will pass by on a train, they say
> All the boys and girls on the reservation
> Will receive pants, skirts and sailor blouses.
> Our parcel arrives from the Indian Agency
> To the foster home where I live.
> There is one sailor blouse, a skirt.
>
> My heart goes flip flop.
> But the fun day goes by
> With no one saying, "Put your blouse on."
> My heart stops.
>
> The day is over
> Gone, my longing to see the King and the Queen.
> And now my foster brother has new handmade pants
> With a sailor blouse to match.
>
> My heart goes flip flop.

In spite of everything, I dearly loved my foster mother in this home. She was always giving me good food and we shared comforting, soothing talks. The only flaw in this was her husband, who had a reputation for hurting children for the sake of his own twisted desires.

I remember suffering abuse at that house, from the man. When the man asked me to do something that was not pleasant and I objected to it, he said, "But you do it so good." That approval meant something to me. When you're in a foster home, you do what you're told. If you're told you're doing something right, you do it again — and again and again, no matter how negative or impossible or bad or ugly it is. And if you get praised for doing it, you want that praise. I always looked for praise and approval when I was little. I hunted for it. If I was bringing in wood for the house and piling it against the stove, and my foster mother said, "Oh, you're a smart little girl and you're very good to do this for me," I would keep on piling that wood, time after time, because I liked the praise. In all my homes, that's what I searched for; that was how I survived. When I was older, I didn't care whether I was praised or not; what I did was my own business. But when I was little, it mattered.

In order to get away from the man who abused me, I would go upstairs in his house. There was a little crawlspace there; the entrance was about as big as my face and head are today — it was not very big. I used to crawl into it and go to the end. Nobody could come after me because nobody could fit in that crawlspace — only me. I used to go as far as I could, and then fall asleep.

Again and again, my love for my foster mother meant so much to me that I was willing to shut my mind to the harm the man inflicted, and hope that things would end with his death. This didn't happen, so the abuse went on for I don't know how long, until I told another little girl, and she told her mother, and the matter was looked into by people on the reservation. Soon I was moved to a different foster home. It broke my heart when my foster mother blamed me for what had happened, although I was only seven years old. I expressed my love for her, but she shut me out with an angry burst of words: "*Mu wela'luksiwun* (You have no gratitude)." I cried and wondered if I should have kept my mouth shut. I missed her love more than anything else.

Many years later, my husband Frank Joe was surprised when he came home and announced that the man in that foster home had died, and I blurted out, "Good riddance!"

"I'm so mad at you for saying that," Frank said. I never did explain to him why I said it. Even today, I feel the release of those words; but when I hear of any child being hurt, the pain returns.

I still have dreams about those times. One night, a few nights ago, I dreamt about a little child in a bed. I had covered that little child. I don't know who she was. It seemed like she was me, but I was also the mother covering the child.

In my dream, someone else came into the room and roughly pulled the covers off the child. I remember telling that person, "How would you like it if somebody did that to your child?"

It's hard for me to describe what it was like when I was little. Words sometimes will not come to me; it's as if they're stuck inside. Some of the hurt was too great, so I just bundled it up and put the little bundles away. Those bundles are still on the shelf today and I cannot open some of them. If I open them, I will cry, I will get hurt. So that's why I leave the bundles alone. It's hard enough to survive knowing that they are there.

■ ■ ■

When I was taken away from the house where I had suffered the abuse, I was placed in another foster home on the same reservation, in Millbrook. The old lady who took care of me there was cross at everybody and swore a lot, but was kind and gentle to me. In her own gruff way, she was good. This lady worked hard and had a garden, and I helped her in every way I could — picking apples, peeling things, making jam and preserves.

I remember once I told her I wasn't feeling well. She gave me some concoction — some medicine — that tasted awful and told me to go to bed and stay put: "Go upstairs and get under those blankets and don't pop your head out!" My bed was straw on the floor covered with a quilt and a lot of old coats. I stayed under the quilt with my head covered, the way I was told to, not looking around — "not even to peek out the window." Eventually I became nauseated and ran to the bucket and vomited a long white worm. I thought I would die for sure. "I'm going to die!" I cried, but the old lady came up the stairs and said, "There's nothing the matter with you. Go to bed and stay under those blankets!" The next day, I was covered with measles from head to foot and soon began to get better. After a couple of days I was allowed up, and I remember being so happy. I didn't like being in that bed; I wanted to be outside, playing and going to school.

While I was with this old lady, I also had a swollen lump on the side of my neck. The lady took me to a doctor and he arranged it so that I would enter the hospital the next day. However, the old lady was supposed to attend the wedding of one of her relatives in the community that day and she couldn't take me to the hospital just then. She dressed me up and told me to stay out of sight, but that is hard to do at a wedding. I was ooh'd and ahh'd at, and called "you poor child" all evening. The poor lady never heard the end of it, all the rest of her life.

Although she was sometimes offensive to others, the old lady was good to me. The only thing she could not control was the hatred one of her sons had for me. Once, I did something wrong when we were sitting at the table. I don't remember what it was; perhaps I just had a snotty nose or something — I did not have proper manners. But the man didn't like to see me sitting across from him at the table, so he ordered me to sit on the second step below the doorway for all my meals. The old lady was good, but this was her Number One son. The lady's husband was sick and the son was the family provider. Whatever he wanted was the law in that house.

It was one of my chores to take care of the old lady's sick husband — emptying his spittoon, tidying his bed, helping with his meals. The husband had tuberculosis and he lived in an extension that had been built onto the house. His room was comfortable and it had a little camp stove. I would fill the stove with wood and, during the day, it was my job to make sure the fire didn't go out. I remember the husband ate good meals, and sometimes he didn't want to eat all his food. He would give me a pork chop or a baked potato or some pie. Sometimes people would tell me, "Don't eat the things he eats, because he has TB." But I had no fear of that; I didn't understand it.

In midsummer of the year that I lived in this home, the old lady and I went to Heatherton, Nova Scotia, to be part of the St. Ann's Day celebration. St. Ann is the grandmother saint of the Mi'kmaq, and her feast is held each year on July 26. On the Sunday following that date, there is the *"Tewa'lud* (Taken Out)" — the ceremony where a statue of St. Ann is taken to the rock where Abbe Maillard, the Apostle of the Mi'kmaq, used to teach. Our people have kept this feast alive since the 1600s. The celebrations are held in different parts of the Maritime provinces where Mi'kmaq are found, but the spot that draws the most people is on Chapel Island in Cape Breton. There is much preparation before the feast day; the people camp out on the Island, with all of their children, for up to four days.

> Her painted image hangs on my wall
> On tanned skin with ragged fringe
> Her kind eyes and gentle mouth
> Remind me of a grandmother
> Who may intercede for me when trouble arises
>
> Her likeness was put into our care long ago
> By long robes. Their teaching told
> That she is the grandmother of *Niskam*
> The *Kji-Saqamow* in the sky.
> We then told our children, the many generations,
>
> With the oral weight we always carry.
> The beautiful St. Ann we love,
> Our *kijinu* in the sky.

My foster mother and I stayed overnight at a friend's house, where I slept with a lot of other little children. In the morning, I could hear two old women talking about somebody who had kept them awake all night, "knocking." Just then, there was a knock on the door and a man asked for my foster mother. "I'm sorry to bring you bad news," he told her.

I remember my foster mother crossed herself and we immediately rushed home.

When we arrived, the old lady's husband was in a coffin. I remember that he had something like a diaper wrapped around his head, from his chin to his forehead. I was told to pay my respects, and I do not recall what I did. Not too long after, I ended up at another foster home.

■ ■ ■

In my new home — again it was in Millbrook Reservation — the man of the house told me to take a chair and sit beside him at the table. He said, "Every time you see Irene" — that was his wife's name — "serve the table, you go get that chair and sit down here." From that day forward, I always grabbed that particular chair — a straight-backed chair — and made sure I sat alongside the man. His two daughters would want that chair, but I would fight for it. I imagine he hadn't liked seeing me eat on the second step at my previous home.

I came to know this man as Uncle Andy and I have respected him throughout my life. One of the daughters in the family is almost the same age as me, and we still talk about when we were little kids and how we used to go swimming and play hooky sometimes, and do other crazy things we weren't supposed to do. This home in Millbrook Reservation was my last foster home before I went to live with my dad for a year, and it was the one I loved most of all. The mom was good to me, and the dad was strict but tolerant.

■ ■ ■

Finally, when I was nine, I got to live for one year with my dad, my brothers Soln and Roddy, and my sister Annabel. (My other brother, Matt, was in residential school until he was sixteen, and then left Whycocomagh with his foster family. Roddy knew him better than any of us because they were at school together; the rest of us did not get a chance to see him very often. For that reason, I never really got to know Matt.)

That year, 1941-42, was the happiest I had ever known. Our extreme poverty meant nothing to me; my family meant everything good and secure. My brothers and sister did what they could to take care of me. It was not the best of care, but the closeness we shared stayed with us always.

I loved my two brothers very much. Soln was very protective of me because I was the *mta'ksn* (baby) in the family. Soln was a good man — a soft-spoken individual who cared for people and was like a father to everybody. He was the loving family member who kept the younger siblings in line, and he was the one I went to with any problem I had. I remember his wise words, so much like my dad's.

Roddy was eight years older than I, and still a happy-go-lucky guy. He and Soln would have friendly talks about everything under the sun. I would listen to them for hours.

My older sister Annabel was not so happy. She had grown up too fast after mom died. Now she was fifteen and pregnant. I was small and didn't know what the fuss was all about. Nobody mentioned to me that she was having a baby, and I didn't know the meaning of her big stomach. All of a sudden she moved away from us, to the house next door. A woman there took care of her.

Later, I found out that Annabel had argued with my dad. He didn't like her situation and he still depended upon her too much. It was just too much responsibility for her. My dad also forbade her to marry the man she loved — he was another Native from Saskatchewan — because he had a different religion. Oh, that broke her heart. So she had a little boy all on her own — next door, away from home. Me, I was crazy over the little fellow. To me, he was my little brother.

One of the things I remember from that year of living with my dad was that he would open a book full of hieroglyphic symbols, and I would look at it with him. He would read from the symbols — any page at all — and he would read them in Mi'kmaq. Later on, when I did my own writing, I came across histories saying that we, the Mi'kmaq, left no word. That would make me so mad. I know there were Mi'kmaq symbols and I know people wrote to each other in Mi'kmaq; my own sister used to receive letters written in Mi'kmaq. Today, when I'm reading about my people, I read between the lines. I know the way my people are; I know what they could and could not have done. So I reason it out: They may have done one thing, and non-Natives saw something else. The non-Natives recorded things as if they saw the truth, but they did not always see the truth. In this way, I always try to reason out my own history from what I know of both sides.

"I noticed children
Making marks with charcoal on the ground,"
Said LeClercq.
"This made me see
That in form would create a memory
Of learning more quickly
The prayers I teach.

"I was not mistaken,
The characters produced
The effect I needed.
For on birchbark they saw
These familiar figures
Signifying a word,
Sometimes two together.
The understanding came quickly
On leaflets
They called *kekin a'matin kewe'l*
Tools for learning.

"The preservation of written word
Was in so much care.
They kept them neatly in little cases
Of birchbark
Beautified with wampum
Of beadwork and quills."
These were the Micmac hieroglyphics
The written word of the Indian
That the world chooses to deny.

I also remember that Christmas with my family. The boys
told me to write down what I wanted; Roddy explained that I
had to write very clearly so that Santa would be able to read what
I wrote. My list was long — it even included a bed for a doll, a
bottle for nursing and a cupboard for dishes. Then I hung up my
stocking. The next morning, I awoke, jumped out of my bed of
quilts on the floor, kicked away the brick we used for heat, and
scrambled down the ladder that led from my attic room. The
whole family looked on as I exclaimed over every gift. Though

the bed and cupboard were made of shingles, they were like treasures to me — and the doll wet herself when I fed her! I remember my dad smiling at all of us lovingly. The time we spent that Christmas lingers in my mind to this day. Even though it had to end, it is a time so precious I hold on to it in memory.

One day in the spring, I heard my brothers arguing about who was the stronger one. Soln was tall and broad-shouldered and slim, while Roddy was skinny and of medium height. They were both trying to enlist in the Armed Forces. Soln came back from his physical with a downcast expression — he had failed because of a broken ear drum. Roddy, the skinny one, was the one who got to enlist.

Soon after that, we were getting ready for Easter and the boys purchased new sneakers and a dress for me. Though the dress probably cost less than a dollar, I thought it and the sneakers were the best in the world. I remember on Easter Sunday I stayed close by my dad's side all day long; maybe I sensed already that he could go at any time.

The Wednesday after Easter, my dad said he felt cold and couldn't seem to get warm. Finally, he was taken to the hospital with pneumonia. On Friday, we were summoned to his bedside in the hospital; Annabel and I went with Chief Joe Julian.

I held my father's cold hand. I remember he told my sister what to do with me. "*Muk kwe'ji li'ewij* Oxford (Do not let your sister go to Oxford)," he warned.

But, in the end, that is exactly what happened to me.

> My body lies upon the grass.
> Peaceful odours of the wood
> And dreams of my people filter past —
> Images of when I was a child,
> My father, my mother,
> A smile present.

My body lay on the earth floor.
Reality came when I awoke,
Breaking the images of ages before.
In a lost fantasy
Desires broke without reason.

Kejitu mu telianukw
Katu welte'tm.

■ ■ ■

When Dad died in 1942, my three brothers, Soln, Roddy and Matt, were twenty-one, eighteen and fourteen. Annabel was fifteen and I was ten. From that time forward, my brothers had little influence over my life, although they tried as much as they could to have contact throughout the years. Roddy went into the army that year, and sent me an allotment of his army pay. In his own way — in the only way he knew how — he tried to help me. The allotment stopped after a few years, but none of us knew until much later that Roddy had been injured in a tank accident. Matt also went into the army, and then to Boston where he took a job at the Boston Indian Council, and I did not see him for a long time. Soln stayed in Millbrook and, after awhile, got married and had a family.

When Dad died, Annabel gave away her little boy to Mary Ann Gould, whose husband was a relation. It was very hard for her to do this, but she was still a child herself. She did not get to marry the Native man from Saskatchewan who was the father of the child. He became a soldier and went overseas, and was killed a few weeks later. I remember that Annabel cried for a long time. After that, she went to live in Membertou Reservation with our stepsister Susie, and later on she got married to a non-Native person and moved to Halifax with him. But she only ever had the one child of her own.

As for me, my father's wishes were not carried out and I ended up in Oxford, Nova Scotia, living with my half brother William and his wife. This was the first non-Native community

I had ever lived in, and it was the first place where I saw heavy drinking. My time there was not all bad, though; it was a learning experience. It's the place I wrote about many years later, in *Poems of Rita Joe*.

My first year in Oxford I had no schooling, but I went back to school in 1944. This was when I found out how the non-Indians act towards Natives. I think I may have experienced this attitude earlier, in Millbrook, but I did not really understand what it meant until I was ten, eleven, twelve, and lived in a non-Native community. There were only three Native families living in Oxford. One family lived four or five miles away from mine, and the other family was about one-quarter of a mile away. I wouldn't say we were considered to be less than animals, but … the animosity was there.

> Need you think
> That I am unaware
> Of others' cold stares —
> The small attempts at communication.
> Do you ever wonder
> Why I am afraid to approach you,
> To express my love
> Of my tradition?

I found that it wasn't *all* negative, though; it depended on us, too. I did make friends with the boys and girls at school, although there was some meanness — more from the boys than the girls. I played ball or played house with the white girls and, if I acted nice towards them, I would be accepted. As long as we were at school, I was one of them, I was no different from them. But they never came to my house and I didn't go to theirs. I was not permitted into their homes or allowed to get too close to them.

This experience of belonging to an alien nation made a permanent impression on me. Even today, I use the method of peaceful confrontation to fight it.

Who are you?
Question from a teacher feared.
Blushing, I stammered
What?

Other students tittered.
I sat down forlorn, dejected,
And made a vow
That day

To be great in all learning,
No more uncertain.
My pride lives in my education,
And I will relate wonders to my people.

■ ■ ■

In Oxford, I soon saw liquor close up; I even learned how to make it. Between 1942 and 1944, I became the best underage home-brew maker in Cumberland County.

My dad had hated liquor, so I didn't have much experience of it. At first, my half brother and his wife, Madeline, hid it from me; but eventually I saw them making it. I remember coming home from school one day and finding my half brother down in the root cellar. I saw that William had a bottle, and I watched him pouring something that looked like tea into this bottle. I didn't know what the liquid was, but I heard him say to Madeline, "Oh, she saw it. You may as well let her know."

They drank openly in front of me after that. My foster mother even showed me how to make it. "You mix it, and then you cover the bottle until it's nice and warm, and it will brew," she told me. It made them feel good to drink, and they would compliment me. "You make such good home-brew," they would say, and I would feel happy to have their approval.

A strange thing about living in that home was that the adults would often go away to work and be gone for two or three days. They would leave word for me to make the home-brew so that it was ready when they returned. And that's how I — someone who detests liquor — became one of the best home-brew makers in the county.

Things happened in my stepbrother's house that are very frightening for a small child. I remember one evening I was all alone and didn't know where the adults had gone. I was supposed to go get bread at the store and put it away for tomorrow's breakfast. So I went to buy the bread and on my way home, as I passed two bushes near where I lived, somebody jumped out at me and pretty nearly caught me. I ran and ran with all of my power and, although normally I would never go into a non-Native home without knocking, this once I was so terrified that I opened the door of the first home I came to and ran inside. Then I stood there, crying. "What's the matter?" the woman of the house asked me. I poured out my heart to this woman, and she kept me there for a while. Then she told her husband to take me home.

The man took me home, but, after he left, I knew that danger was still out there. I sat at the kitchen table, not moving. I was terrified. *What if the man from the bushes comes after me?* I thought. *I don't know what to do. I'm trapped in a corner; there is only one door. What if I can't get out?* I sat there, petrified, for a long time. Suddenly, the door opened and a man in an army uniform came walking in. It was a relative who happened to be coming home from the war. Oh, I was so glad to see him. I just sat there, shaking and terrified, and he sat down beside me. "What's the matter, Rita?" he asked.

I said, "I'm afraid to go upstairs to sleep. I'm sleepy but I'm afraid to go upstairs." I was in a panic. The man comforted me and gently said, "Dear, you go up to bed." So I went upstairs and crawled into bed and went straight to sleep on my straw mattress on the floor. I'll never forget how afraid I was. A lot of things like that happened while I lived in my half brother's house.

On another occasion, my foster mother told me to drink the home brew. "No," I protested. "I don't like it."

"If you don't drink it," she said, "I'll throw you out of the house. Get the hell out!" So I put the bottle near my mouth and pretended to drink.

I swallowed the home-brew only once; it was my foster mother who made me drink it. The alcohol made me vomit. Oh,

I was miserable. It was wintertime, but I was sick and miserable, so I took the quart and went outside into a field and rolled myself in a quilt and lay on the ground. I lay there, puking; I remember being warm.

Again, it was a soldier coming home from the war who rescued me; this time, the soldier was Madeline's son from an earlier marriage, Frank Louis. I must have fallen asleep, because the next thing I remember, the soldier was shaking me. "Come on, get up," he said, and he unrolled me from the quilt and took me into the house. I heard him asking his mother, "Why is she all rolled up in a quilt lying in the snow?"

"I don't know," his mother said. I remember that the solider was very upset about what he had found, and my stepbrother William was in no shape at all to talk about it. There were angry words, back and forth. Finally, everybody got it into their heads that they would go on a trip to Truro. The train was due to arrive in a couple of hours, so we got dressed and forgot about the problem. By that time, I was all right. The soldier heated up some soup for me and made me eat it. Then we all got on the train and went to Truro.

The soldier was angry with his mother for a long time afterwards, though. I heard him say to her, "Don't ever let me come home and see that child in that shape again."

In the quiet loss of dignity
I run to escape my problem
The alcoholic load I use as a crutch,
My body numb
And the loud noise I hear in the mind
My insides bind
My life a mess, moving onward blind

I need a foundation like long ago
Where everything depended on survival
And our nation grew
Love and strength multiplied the gifts
To my person now due

···

A lasting impression remains in my mind of a teacher in Oxford Junction. She was strict but kind. I still have a memory of her standing near my home, watching, as I pulled a sleigh full of wood. It was Christmas Day. My foster parents were away in Springhill, where they had gone shopping the day before; they had promised to be back, but I found myself alone when I woke up. My stocking, and the Christmas tree I had found and trimmed and stood on a chair, had yielded nothing. I cried my tears until there were no more, then passed time getting wood ("for therapy," as I look at it today). On one of my dozen trips, the teacher was standing there with a box in her hand. "Santa lost his way," she said.

After my discovery that morning, I no longer believed in Santa Claus, but I accepted the gift. The teacher's eyes crinkled as she smiled at me. I took the box with my heart full of love for this woman, and I always remember what she did. Today, I think that perhaps the people in the community knew what was going on. Their gossip may have brought me sympathy.

···

Sometimes, the family would ask me if I wanted to go to the Indian Residential School; I always said no. I tried to say what I thought they wanted me to say. I was like that with all my foster parents — I said what I thought they wanted to hear, in order to make everybody happy. I remember that, once, an Indian agent and a Mountie even came looking for me and I was told to crawl under a couch and hold my breath. I lay there as still as I could for a long time.

Finally, a time arrived when I felt I had to get away from Oxford Junction. It was 1944 and I was twelve years old. My half brother was a hardworking man but his drinking was frightening. As well, I wanted to learn how to cook and sew. I remember watching Madeline make baskets, but she wouldn't teach me how it was done. I wanted to learn these and other things. I also knew that my dad had not wanted me to stay in Oxford because he knew about the drinking, and, to this day, I feel that my dad's spirit had something to do with my leaving. I don't know what would have happened if I had stayed on.

In May of that year, my half brother went away for a time, to work in Halifax, and Madeline was left all alone to take care of me. One day, a woman from Millbrook came to visit Madeline, and the two of them decided to go picking mayflowers. The next day, they put the mayflowers in little bundles and sold them. It went so well, they decided to do the very same thing the following week.

That's when I wrote a letter to the Indian Agent in Shubenacadie, Mr. H. C. Rice. I asked him to please come next Wednesday and take me to Indian Residential School, because that was the day my foster mother would be away picking mayflowers. After the letter was written, I went to the corner store and confided in the storekeeper. Her name was Mrs. Rogers — I'll never forget it. She helped me address an envelope to Mr. Rice.

By the time the next Wednesday came, I had forgotten about the letter and gone to school. At recess we were playing ball — I remember I was on third base — when we saw a car arriving in the school driveway. A tall Mountie stepped out of the car, along with a man in a big hat and a business suit. We children all looked at each other, asking, "Who broke a window? Did someone steal apples? What did we do wrong?" Then I heard my name being called and, with a thumping heart, I ran over to my teacher. The man who had come with the Mountie put his arm around my shoulder. "Do you know who I am?" he asked. I just looked up at him. "I'm Mr. Rice," he said. "I came on Wednesday, like you asked." I was fit to be tied, I was so excited.

Mr. Rice talked to the teacher for a bit, then we got into his car. I was thrilled to be riding in the car with the Indian Agent and the Mountie. We drove over to my house, where I found the key under the mat, unlocked the door and went in. "Just take what you have on," Mr. Rice told me. "And take your comb and any other little things you have, but don't take anything else." I gathered up my purse, which contained a comb and a few pennies — my little junk, I called it. As we were about to leave, I noticed that there was a pile of clothes on the floor. "I'm supposed to soak these, sir," I said. "I was told to soak them in the washtub."

"You don't have to soak them," Mr. Rice told me.

"I have to," I said.

"No, you don't," he said. "I say so. Just get in the car." So I got into the car.

First, we drove over to the corner store, and the Mountie explained to Mrs. Rogers what was happening. Then we went to the post office, and the Mountie and Mr. Rice left a letter there for my foster mother. I don't know what they wrote, but I imagine they must have told her that I was going to the Shubenacadie Indian Residential School. Finally, we drove out of town and onto the highway. A short time afterwards, I could see a taxi coming towards us, with two women in the back: Madeline and her friend. I recognized the women right away, and jerked my head down, under the seat. "What's the matter?" Mr. Rice asked. I told him, and he said, "So keep your head down!"

The trip to the Shubenacadie Indian Residential School did not take long. We dropped the Mountie off along the way, and I remember we had a flat tire somewhere around Wentworth. Mr. Rice got out of the car and fixed the tire. We stopped in Truro and Mr. Rice bought me dinner, and a chocolate bar for dessert. "Don't touch that chocolate bar until you've finished all your dinner," he told me. "It's a treat."

Then he phoned ahead to the school, to tell them we would be arriving soon.

■ ■ ■

Many moons have passed since we stood on the shore
Waving to the people on ships going home.
Their gifts of pretty trinkets and pretty beads
I held close to my heart,
And their promises to return and stay with us
Working side by side.

They returned and brought others, so many more,
Until we felt closed in, trying to learn their way.
Adaptation became impossible.
They cleared much land, their buildings tall,
Monuments of their heroes standing in the midst
Of the stone wigwams that reach the sky.

I want to see the clouds but the stones are in my way.
I want to walk the well-worn trails
But the stones hurt my moccasined feet.
I sweat in the close spaces, my brow misty with memories
The picture on my mind a wigwam
With laughing children, my language spoken by everyone.
My clothes are heavy, so different.
I want to cry, but that is not our way.
The gifts of pretty trinkets
And the pretty beads I hold
The promise still beating the heart.
Why do I feel so alone?
I clutch the pretty beads and trinkets.

Several years ago, when my husband Frank Joe was still alive,
I found out that some of the nuns who had taught at the Shubenacadie Indian Residential School were living in Halifax. I had
thought all of them had died, but my friend Isobel Shea, who
wrote about the school in her book Out of the Depths, told me
that she had talked to a couple of the nuns. When I found that
out, I said to my husband, "Let's go see the nuns. I want to meet
them again." I phoned ahead to one of them I knew, Sister
Justinian. She had been one of my favourite nuns at the school.

When I walked into her room, Sister Justinian put out her
arms for me, and I went into them. She was over eighty years old,
and she cried. I cried buckets, too. I think she had heard too many
negative stories about the school — all the nuns heard the negative stories. It was true that many negative things occurred, but
there was also a lot of good that happened.

My husband had come with me. He had attended the school
for a little while, too, but at a different time than I had. When we

first met Sister Justinian, Frank talked negatively and tried to vent his emotions. I kept snapping at him, in Mi'kmaq, "Frank, shut up! They're old now. We've got to forgive and forget." When Frank had finally finished his tirade, compassion came over him. "Sister, I don't hate you," he told her. "It's just that I was hurt so much when I was in there, and Rita was hurt and a lot of us were hurt. Some of us didn't have fathers or mothers, and when you knock down people like that, they become demoralized."

Me, I have always had some sympathy for the nuns. Often when I say this, people are surprised because they have heard a lot of stories about the place. Yes, I had some negative experiences. We were not allowed to express our Native language, culture and spirituality, and these things are very important to us. Some of us carry that on our shoulders still; our anger is still there. But I do not like to dwell on the negative if I can help it. The positive outlook that I have worked on for so long now turns me off the negative. I look for the good. For instance, I had a friend in the school — a nun who worked with me in the laundry. She gave me inspiration. Every morning before our chores, she would dig in the deep pocket of her habit and give me a hard candy or some other small gift. I looked forward to this, to see what she would produce next. It is like a "trinkets and beads" story, except it meant something to her as well as to me.

I had a long talk with my friend Isobel Shea when she was writing her book. I asked her why she called it *Out of the Depths*. "That's the prayer we used to recite, Isobel," I said.

She said, "Yes, do you remember when we were in school? We used to pray, 'Out of the depths I have cried to thee, O Lord. Lord, hear my voice.' Well, I wanted to leave the school and be taken away from that unhappy environment and I prayed and prayed and prayed and kept using that prayer. And it didn't come about; I stayed there until I was sixteen, like we all did."

She told me, "The reason I wrote that book was to heal the people who were in there. There's a lot of healing that has to be done. Many negative feelings that we carry around are because of that place."

I said, "Isobel, you have to write a sequel to it, and tell some of the positive things."

"All right, Rita," she replied. "My challenge is right here: Think of one good story you can tell about that place." So there we sat, in a room with a tape recorder between us, and it was a long while before I could bring up a good story.

"See," Isobel said. "We remember so much of the bad that happens to us, it's hard to dig up the good."

Still, today, I do not regret going into the residential school. A few years ago, someone in my community made fun of me in front of an audience. "Rita put herself in that place," she said, and she laughed. Some other people laughed, too. But there was another individual in the group who said, "Rita had bundles of hurt to carry when she was little, so she put herself in there for safekeeping." The explanation for what I did is all there, in those words.

Today on television I heard a discussion
Of residential schools across the country.
I saw a man talk about sex abuse done to him
He even had a hard time saying it.
I was in one of the schools, my daughter too.
There was physical abuse where I was
Not sex, but mind mistreatment.
With me, there was one individual who did this
As always there are certain people who do.
The rest of the nuns were tolerable
The priest in my time a kind man.

My daughter says she didn't have it hard
But again only one person did her wrong
And upon seeing her in later years
This person hugged her and cried.
My daughter knew the forgiving song.

I know for a fact people who came from schools
Have turned into productive persons.
Even women who had it hard have become nuns
And men from across the country their dreams realized.
In my case I've nobody to blame for being there.
I put myself where I would receive training.

The four years have given me strength.
My life to this day has gained courage.
I know who I am, and my people are the prize.

■ ■ ■

When I arrived at the Shubenacadie Indian Residental School, the priest and the nuns came out to greet me. I remember how I felt walking into that place. To me, the school looked like a castle: the ornamented door, the shiny waxed floors, the pictures on the walls and curtains on the windows. It was so beautiful and elegant, and so different from living in the foster homes, with their poor conditions. I felt moved.

The nuns took me downstairs to the recreation room, where they examined my hair. It was long and wavy, but when they finished examining me, they cut it short with bangs. I was given a uniform and told to take a bath, and then an older girl was assigned to take care of me. She took me out to meet the hundred or so girls who lived there.

I was like a celebrity to the other girls. They asked me all kinds of questions: "Where did you come from?" "What were you doing?" Some of them just stared at me.

When I told them that I had put myself into the school, many of them looked at me in disbelief and said, "Are you crazy?" I didn't know why they would consider me crazy. Later, I found out the reasons.

All in all, the four years I spent in the school were memorable. Most of the nuns were kind. The priest, Father Brown, was from Cumberland County and the fact that we were both from the same area cemented our friendship. He was a gentle man. I only heard him raise his voice once, when he was angry that one of the girls had been severely beaten.

It is true that bad things happened while I was there. You can't help having a chip on your shoulder if you are told, military style, when to go to the bathroom, when to eat, when to do this and that, when to pray. We were even told when to yawn and cough. Children can't help themselves when they cough, but we were told, "Stop your barking!" That's a negative thing to hear when you are a child coughing, not barking like a dog.

Not all of the nuns were mean, though, and a few were very kind. I remember there was one who worked in the sewing room with us and taught us to sew. Sister Rita we called her. We all loved Sister Rita. We used to talk to her and try to pump her, try to get her to tell us stories. "What were you like when you were small?" we would ask. "Did you play like all little girls?"

"Oh, yes," she'd tell us. "I used to be a tomboy. I'd climb trees and swim." She would tell us these stories and we loved her because she did not look down on us and she taught us what we were supposed to learn. She even befriended us.

That's also the way it was with the sister who worked in the laundry with me. Every day, she would have a candy or a chocolate or a little gift — perhaps a notebook or pencil or box of crayons. They were simple little gifts, but to me there were very important. This nun was like a mother figure to me, and I loved her. I still love her today.

■ ■ ■

They say that I must live
A white man's way.
This day and age
Still being bent to what they say,
My heart remains
Tuned to native time.

We prayed a lot in the school. In the morning, one of the sisters would come into our dormitory and clap. Her clapping would wake us up, and we would kneel down near our beds on the cold floor. There were one hundred girls in our dorm, which was on one side of a long hall, and there were one hundred boys in a dorm on the other side. The door to the hallway was shut during the night and we were all locked into our dormitories. There was a fire escape, but I often wondered what would have happened if there was a fire.

Each morning after we had prayed, we'd get up, get dressed, fix our beds, get into line. Everything had to be done in a military style — we were in line for everything. We'd all march downstairs to the washroom. There were about thirty sinks and fourteen stalls. We would wash and try to use the mirror to make ourselves pretty. Then we'd get into line again and go to church for forty-five minutes. After that, we'd go into the dining room, eat, come out and go to our jobs. We had about half an hour to do our jobs; everybody had a specific place to go each day, and everybody had a specific task. Then the first bell would ring and we would finish up our work and head for the classroom. Five minutes later the final bell would ring and, by then, we had to be sitting at our desks.

At dinner time we would get in line again. After we ate, we'd have a few minutes to play hopscotch or other games outside. Certain people would do the dishes. Then there would be school again in the afternoon.

I remember, when I was about fourteen, I worked in the kitchen a lot. For that, you had to get up at four in the morning. We'd bake bread and — oh my God — every second day we'd bake about thirty-five or forty loaves. Holy Lord! And we made soup in a huge pot that was very high and very round. We'd make porridge in the morning, in a big, big porridge pot and we'd boil over two hundred eggs. It was a lot of hard work that we did in the kitchen, and the cook could be cruel.

In our classes, we were taught pottery, and how to sew clothes and make things. We were also taught how to knit, but one thing I didn't learn while I was there was how to crochet. Only special girls were allowed to crochet; these special girls could make all their clothes, knit sweaters *and* crochet.

I remember that we would make socks for the army. We'd have a great big box full of socks to ship away — a couple of hundred pairs. Everybody was knitting socks. You'd be given about a week to knit a pair out of brown yarn. That's when I learned how to knit. I could knit socks — or mittens, or whatever — in the dark.

I didn't mind the teaching I received in that school, I just wish there had been more of it. In my Grade Five classroom, if you were able to get your work done before two o'clock, you were allowed to go to the library — they called it the "reading room." It was right next door to my classroom and, oh, I wanted to be in that library! My goodness! For days, I would get my work done and sit quietly at my desk, and finally one day the teacher said to me, "You can go in there."

There they were: books of knowledge. I just grabbed the first book I came to, I was in such a hurry to read anything. I remember that I got hold of one about astronomy and the stars and the moon. I was fascinated by that book. From that time on, I worked hard to have the freedom of reading and about once a week I would be allowed to go into that room.

The reading room was always kept locked, and it was where the nuns would put the Christmas parcels that came from home. As Christmas approached, new boxes would arrive in the reading room every day. The mail would be delivered and someone would announce, "That's your parcel there. And so-and-so's parcel is there, and so-and-so has two parcels." We would compare: "How big is your parcel? Oh, it's only a little box!"

During each of the four years I was at the school, I looked for a parcel from home. But no parcel came until I was fifteen. I used to voice my feelings to the nun I was working with in the laundry. "Do you have any brothers or sisters?" she asked me once. I told her, "Yeah, I've got a brother in the army in England somewhere. I don't know where he is. And another brother's in the army, too, and I don't know where my oldest brother is right now, either. My half brother does not communicate with me at all. And my sister, she has her problems, I guess."

Finally, when I was fifteen, I was told, "Rita, there's a parcel there for you."

"Where did it come from?" I asked.

"We don't know, there's no name on it."

I remember I was so happy to receive this parcel, and so anxious to see who it was from. But when I opened it there was no name inside, and I couldn't make out the postmark. It contained fruit and candies, a handkerchief, hand lotion and pretty pins for my hair. Oh, I treasured those gifts. They meant so much to me. Of course, after the holidays I told my friend the nun about them. "I got a parcel this year," I said, "and I got all this stuff, but I don't know who gave it to me, there's no name!"

"Oh," she said, "somebody must care for you." She never took credit for the parcel; she wanted me to feel good. I just told her how much I appreciated whoever had given it to me.

Another thing that meant a lot to me was skating in the wintertime. Every year, I wanted skates. There were a lot of skis and sleighs to play with, and certain people had skates too. The nun who was in charge of the recreation favoured certain people — they were her pets and the rest of us were less than frogs! I didn't get skates until I was fourteen or fifteen years old. I was so happy then. After school, I'd take those skates and go to the pond and skate till five o'clock.

In the summertime — in June — a lot of the children would go home. There were about a hundred girls during the school year, but about seventy would go home in the summer. During the four years I lived in the Shubenacadie Residential School, I never went home, summer or winter. I envied the children who could.

The nuns tried to treat us a little better in the summer. For example, all through the school year we wouldn't get cornflakes for breakfast, except maybe on Christmas or at Easter. But in the summer we'd have cornflakes and juice every morning. We'd go swimming — the nuns would pack us into a truck and take us to the water — and we'd go berry picking and have picnics. We'd always have lots of toys to play with because there were only thirty of us and we didn't have to fight over them. The nuns would try to give us treats and fill our time — so that we wouldn't be lonesome, I imagine. And they were a little more lenient in the summer. We could wander away from the school — but not too far — and sometimes we'd be allowed to sleep in. We didn't have to go to church as often, either.

During the school year, many of the children would have regular visits from their relatives. My brother Soln came occasionally, but mostly I didn't have visitors. The way I used to think of it was like this: I knew a lot of people from different reserves, so if somebody had a mother or a father or a cousin coming to visit them, I often knew who their relations were. I could talk to them about who I knew and, in that way, I would get to have a little portion of the visit, too.

It is like that with everything in my life. I look for an honourable image to create. Sometimes — with many things that happened at school — I have had to search for a long time, but when I find it, it is good.

> I lost my talk
> The talk you took away
> When I was a little girl
> At Shubenacadie school.
>
> You snatched it away;
> I speak like you
> I think like you
> I create like you
> The scrambled ballad, about my word.
>
> Two ways I talk
> Both ways I say,
> Your way is more powerful.
>
> So gently I offer my hand and ask,
> Let me find my talk
> So I can teach you about me.

■ ■ ■

I left the school when I was sixteen.

It was June 1948, and I had finished Grade Eight. The day before I was to leave, two nuns took me aside and invited me into the office. They said, "We have two options for you. We have one place where we can send you, in British Columbia. You can finish high school there and then go to college. It is possible you could become a nun like us. We've been observing you for four years now, and we think you are good with children." They gave me many compliments.

Then they said, "Or, we have a job lined up for you at the Halifax Infirmary."

"The job! I'd like the job!" I replied. I didn't want to become a nun; I was aching to have my freedom. I was not nun material, in my own eyes. For a whole year after I first came out of residential school, I never went near a church. I misplaced the anger I felt about the regimentation of spiritual life in that school.

The day after announcing that I wanted to go to the infirmary, I got on the train to Halifax. I wore an ankle-length skirt and a blouse, and I was given one extra skirt, one extra blouse and two sets of underwear.

At first, as the train pulled away, I cried. The place had been my foster home for four years. I was just sixteen and I felt insecure and unsure of myself, and all on my own. But I also felt freedom. I made a vow to myself that nobody was going to tell me what to do again. I was finally grown up, and nobody would ever hurt me again; nobody would ever tell me when to eat, wash, go to bed or go to the bathroom. Most of all, the spiritual part of me would be my own. If I was going to commit a sin, I would commit it with my own free will.

The confinement of my will had been going on for so long that I cried just until the school was out of sight. Then I began to giggle — and I sat there, giggling, to my heart's content.

■ ■ ■

Many, many years later, the Shubenacadie school was about to be torn down. My husband and I heard about this and went to take a look at it.

By now, the school building was old. The bricks were still standing but the windows were all broken. Inside, the plaster and pipes were falling. It was a misery to look at.

We went around to the entrance at the back. My husband said he remembered hauling wood and coal through the back entrance when he was very young. He couldn't go through that door. He had a feeling of severe oppression, as if someone was telling him, "Get out, get out, get out."

We talked about this for a bit, and I said, "Maybe the spirits of the children who have died here are trying to warn us not to go in there. They hate this building in their hearts." While I lived there, spirits roamed the school building and we children had a lot of encounters with them. Today, I think of spirits that appear anywhere on this earth as being the result of trauma. If there was trauma in a building, the spirits associated with the trauma would live there. Over the years, so much trauma had happened in the residential school — so many people were hurt — that it played itself over and over again through the spirits.

I looked through the doorway of the school but didn't go all the way inside. Finally, I told Frank I would meet him at the road. I walked alone around the outside of the building. When I got to the other side, I saw a woman — a stranger — standing there. She said, "I'm afraid the building is dangerous and you must not go in. I've come to warn you to stay away."

I did stay away, too. That was the last time I ever saw that school.

> If you are on Highway 104
> In a Shubenacadie town
> There is a hill
> Where a structure stands
> A reminder to many senses
> To respond like demented ones.
>
> I for one looked in the window
> And there on the floor
> Was a deluge of misery
> Of a building I held in awe
> Since the day
> I walked in the ornamented door.
>
> There was grime everywhere
> As in buildings left alone or unused.
> Maybe to the related tales of long ago
> Where the children lived in laughter, or abuse.

I had no wish to enter
Nor to walk the halls.
I had no wish to feel the floors
Where I felt fear
A beating heart of episodes
I care not to recall.
The structure stands as if to say:
I was just a base for theory
To bend the will of children
I remind
Until I fall.

SONG OF MY YOUTH
(1950 — 1968)

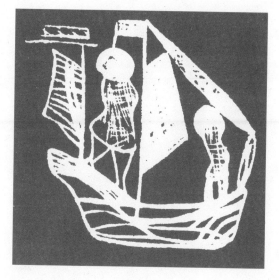

EPITE'S

My moccasin trod on lonely trails,
I needed to learn about life
Where my country failed.
I made them see I never died
My emblems withstood the flood
The twisted tried.

Leaving residential school I felt free, but my spirits dropped as soon as I arrived in Halifax. There was someone waiting for me at the station and she took me directly to the Halifax Infirmary, where I was to work. The place was run by nuns. Right away I again did as I was told and worked as hard as I could. The Indian girls at the infirmary were friendly; the others were okay. I made friends with everybody and tried not to step on toes. It was important to work in a friendly atmosphere, so we created just that.

My first pay really was my own, though. Nobody could take it from me; it was mine! At first, I had only a few clothes, so I washed them every day in order to have clean ones the next day. I did that until I got my first paycheque. Then I bought clothes and a pair of bright red shoes. That was my first purchase: the red shoes. I had wanted to buy something that would be just for me, and I felt so good wearing them — they were the colour I liked and they were all mine.

When I came out of residential school, I was fully developed physically. One of the girls at the infirmary even told me, "I think you need a bra." At school, we had made our underwear out of folded flour bags and elastic snaps, and we were flat. That was the way the nuns had wanted us to be: flatchested, with our hair cut short. I had to learn through experience the use of make-up, hairspray, different shampoos. I was also skinny, tall and awkward. I felt uncomfortable — I thought I was too tall and too skinny. I used to envy the girls who were shorter than me. They would look at me and say, "Gosh, you're so tall. I wish I was like you," and tell me to carry myself with pride, but it took me a long time to accept my height.

In Halifax, I had contact with boys other than my brothers for the first time. When boys said something to me or looked at me, I would be surprised by their flirting. We hadn't been allowed to go near the boys at school. The most we did was throw notes at them that said, "I love you." Real contact with boys went to my head and I had sad experiences and sad realizations. Growing up, I had not received many expressions of love. Now, here were people who seemed to want me. I became a willing partner in what I thought were expressions of love. It took a while for the understanding to sink into my head that these people weren't really interested in me; they were fooling me. I was very naïve — how could you be more naïve than I was, with no father or mother to tell me what to expect? I was often hurt by my experiences with boys and I'd confide my troubles in my friends. Sometimes I'd cry myself to sleep.

I experienced the attitude of non-Native boys towards Natives, too. I remember one time when three of us girls were walking along Barrington Street in Halifax. I had a light complexion when I was sixteen (although, now that I am old, I have ruddy skin). I was light-skinned and I had long brown hair, and I remember I was carrying a purse with a big brass buckle. One of my friends was very dark and had pitch black hair. We walked past a bunch of boys on the street, and somebody called out, "Squaw!"

We stopped dead. "Who are you calling 'squaw'?" I asked.

One of the boys — a big guy, he looked like a college kid — answered, "Not you. The one in the middle."

Before he had even finished speaking, I swung my purse at him. "If you're calling my friend a squaw, we're all squaws, because we're all Native," I said. Oh, we let him have it.

> If words touch me unkindly
> The deeds I fling to the winds.
> Though my heart lies uncaring briefly
> The spirit rises in anger.

So I trim myself to the storm
Until it melts away.
Then I put my best foot forward
Breeding me the woman of stone

And brush away the vacant trivia.
Firmly rooted,
The touching has not yet
Blemished my heart completely.

■ ■ ■

Although my family members can't remember me ever drinking liquor, I did have experience with alcohol when I was sixteen, seventeen, eighteen. Today, my children look at me and say, "Not you, Ma!" but I had some hard years after I came out of school. There were times when I drowned myself in liquor and was the worst that I could be.

Once, I asked a friend, "What do I act like when I'm drunk?" I knew some people have a different personality when they're drinking and I didn't want to be like that.

"Oh, you're the same old jolly, kind Rita," my friend told me. I wasn't a committed drinker — I actually hated the stuff — but I did want to be part of the crowd. For a while I just let loose.

One day in early spring, not even a year after I had left the residential school, I received a letter from one of the nuns. She asked me to come speak to the next group of graduates and tell them what life was like outside the school. I showed the letter to the other Indian girls. "Look at what they want me, a *bad womani'sk*, to do. They want me to talk to the girls, poor things!" I said. That's what we Indian women called ourselves if we went around with the boys — "*bad womani'sk*." I made fun of myself to my friends; I even laughed out loud, and the others laughed too. But the laugh sounded hollow to my ears.

I kept that nun's letter for many years, but, at the time, I was unhappy with what I had become so I didn't answer it. I thought, "I can't go talk to the girls. When I speak to a person, my eyes are direct and open. If I talk to these girls, I'll have to avert my eyes. I can't tell them the truth because they are my people, they are my sisters. And they are pure and good and still innocent. How can I speak to them?" I considered myself to be spoiled.

Eventually, I did go to see the girls at the school, but in my own time and without anybody's invitation. I wore my red, red shoes and a beautiful dress. My hair was long and I had lipstick on, about an inch thick. I wanted to show the nuns: "This is me. You have nothing to do with it, with the way I look or present myself. You have nothing to say about it. I dare you to say anything about it." That was the attitude I had.

In my own language, I explained the hardships Native people experience with the white majority. I pitied the students because they had so much hope for when they got out of school. Already, I knew the losing game of having little education and being a minority. I told them it was hard outside, that education was important. Without a good education, you could not get a good job. I tried to explain what it was like for me outside the school. I told them that it was best to be back on the reservation — you could be safe, if you had relatives there. Some of the girls were like me, without close relatives on the reserve. So I tried to explain the pitfalls of being on your own, and the misery of being naïve.

I didn't like going back to the school at all. The place had bad memories for me. After that, I stayed away.

■ ■ ■

Your buildings, tall, alien,
Cover the land;
Unfeeling concrete smothers, windows glint
Like water to the sun.
No breezes blow
Through standing trees;
No scent of pine lightens my burden.

At the Halifax Infirmary I worked from seven in the morning till seven at night. It was backbreaking work. Every two weeks I was paid fifteen dollars. Even in 1948, that was not much money. I would take the fifteen dollars and buy all the things that I needed, and then ration myself until the two weeks was up. It was hard and I felt like I couldn't get ahead.

Eventually, I got tired of the infirmary job, and one of my friends told me I could work as a waitress and earn more money through tips. So I tried the restaurant trade. At first, the best job I could get was in the kitchen, but after a while I worked my way up to being a waitress. I learned that you have to take all kinds of abuse when you're a waitress. Once, I poured hot soup on top of a man's head. He was a smart alec; he said something very unkind to me. I got fired, of course, and had to look for another job right away.

Around that time, I fell for a young man in Halifax and went to Montreal with him, but I soon came back home again, alone. It was then that I found out I was pregnant. I went to live with my sister, Annabel, who by now also lived in Halifax with her husband. "That's what you get for not listening to me!" Annabel said.

I knew that I had made a big mistake. I had rebelled against the regimentation I had experienced at the Shubenacadie school and thought I could do anything; I thought I was my own boss. I had created my own problems and now I had to find a way to solve them. For a couple of months I worked and worked — washing dishes, waiting on tables, collecting tips and hoping for a better tomorrow.

Annabel's husband, John Ginter, was a non-Native and a good man. He called me his "star boarder," and while I lived with him we would have friendly arguments of a spiritual nature. When my little boy, Eddy, was born in 1949, John and Annabel adopted him. They were good to him, and he grew up knowing Annabel as his mother and John as his father. Sometimes, I reproach myself for giving Eddy away, but I know his welfare was uppermost in my mind at the time. I'm glad he had a stable family, and he has turned out to be a good man.

Soon after Eddy was born, I made another mistake and became pregnant again. When I found this out, I decided I had to get away from Halifax. I wanted to be able to look after myself, I wanted something better, and I did not want anybody — not even Annabel — to tell me what to do.

Once in a while, I would receive letters from my brother Matt. He was now in Boston and he wrote about the good jobs there. My sister Annabel rejected my desire to go to Boston and try to better myself. "You're too young to go," she would say. But I bided my time and saved a little bit of money out of each paycheque.

■ ■ ■

Finally, the day arrived when I had saved enough money to leave Halifax. I sent away for my Indian status card, which meant I only had to pay one-quarter of the usual train fare. After the ticket was paid, I remember I had fifteen dollars left. I packed my gray, cardboard suitcase with my most beautiful clothes, all ironed and neat because I wanted to apply for a job as soon as I got to Boston, before I began to look too pregnant. Then I boarded the train.

Of course, the customs officer at the border made a mess of my suitcase. He just threw everything around — all my beautiful clothes. At first I felt let down, but then I noticed that the man in the next aisle was having a harder time with documentation than I was — my Indian status card earned me both critical appraisal and reluctant permission to proceed. My heart and spirit were hanging by a thread as I passed through the countryside near the border: I was leaving Canada and the familiar territory I had always known.

I arrived in Boston at nine the next morning. The first thing I did was try to buy a newspaper with Canadian money, but nobody would take my dimes or quarters. My country isn't all it's cracked up to be, I thought to myself. Americans won't even take its money! Finally, I flagged a taxi and told the driver to drop me at the nearest bank. I was very ignorant and naïve — as it turned out, the bank was just around the corner and I easily could have walked. I ran inside and told the clerk to hurry and make the exchange — the meter was running. Luckily, there were no other customers in the bank and the clerk did the transaction in a rush. Once exchanged, my money came to all of twelve dollars; I was disappointed all over again. I ran out and paid the taxi driver, and after that I walked everywhere.

My letdown did not last for long. I bought a newspaper and found a hostel for girls where I could get a room for a dollar a night. I asked a police officer how to get to this place and he waved me in the right direction. I found the hostel, showered, changed my clothes and went straight to the employment office. By one o'clock that afternoon, I had a job.

I was lucky at the employment agency. The woman must have pitied me when I announced I had just arrived from Canada that morning. There I was, still a very young woman — eighteen years old, fresh-faced, a naïve Native. I didn't know yet that the situation in Boston was the same as in Halifax: You could try to get a good-paying job, but without the proper education it was not easy. I told the woman I wanted a place where I could sleep and eat and she quickly found me a position at a private hospital in the Beacon Hill district.

I accepted the job right away — I was just happy to be able to stand on my own two feet. I immediately went out to Beacon Hill and was shown my duties. I had to clean rooms, hallways and the kitchen, set up trays, and complete any other chores the supervisor asked of me. My hours were from 7 am to 4 pm and the rest of the time was my own. My room in the hospital residence was beautiful; the sun's rays on the wall mirrored my mood.

■ ■ ■

I didn't have to start work at the hospital until the next morning, so the rest of the day was mine. I decided to look for my brother Matt, who, according to his last letter, lived at 31 Upton Street. "Where is Upton Street, sir?" I asked a police officer, and was told it was on the South Side.

The streets on the South Side of Boston did not look as clean as those in Beacon Hill, but it did not matter to me — I was looking for Matt. At 31 Upton, I found an apartment building and saw a man coming out of it. "Sir, do you know Matthew Bernard?" I asked him.

"Oh, the Professor!" he answered.

"I don't know what you mean," I said.

"That's the nickname we've given him," the man explained. "Go into the basement part of the building and ask the people there."

In the basement, I knocked on a door and a Native woman opened it. "I'm looking for Matt Bernard," I told her.

"He left yesterday on a plane for Halifax, Canada," she answered. Oh my God! I thought to myself. My brother and I have passed each other, going in opposite directions! I had been depending on Matt being in Boston when I arrived. A few years later he came back to Boston and continued with his job as a secretary at the Boston Indian Council — he had learned typing and shorthand after finishing his war service. For now, though, I was alone. The woman invited me in when she saw my surprised face and I explained that I was Matt's sister.

I soon learned all about my brother from his friends who lived in the apartment. "Why do you call my brother a professor?" I asked. I was told that Matt used "high-falutin' words."

I was glad to meet Matt's friends, and I was happy to find some of my own people — the camaraderie was instant. I tried to converse with them in Mi'kmaq, to impress them, but they made fun of my pronunciation of certain words. Sometimes my sounds would be too long, sometimes they'd be too short. I just laughed along with them, happy to have found friends.

At the end of the afternoon, another woman who lived in the apartment arrived home from work and joined us. "Oh my God!" I thought. "She must be eight months pregnant — and she's working!" Then I remembered that I was in a similar situation, and I felt a little more hopeful about keeping my new job.

Soon it was time to go back to Beacon Hill. "Let me take you home," a young Indian man offered. A happy exchange of words followed, and I was told to visit often.

It felt good to walk home with a person of my own age. When I got to my room, I lay on my bed thinking of him; I wished I had met him before my pregnancy. And then I wondered again how long I would last on the job.

> I know we are different
> Though we try to be like you.
> We live in a world of make-believe
> In the field or forest, desk or loom.
> We live in your world of speed and roar
> Of mental energy, and tomorrow's door.
>
> We live, not on a reservation
> Or amongst our people.
> We survive, at the edge of overman
> Trying to do what is right
> In Maine, USA *na ni'n Ni'kmawa'j*
> I am a Micmac.

■ ■ ■

I was eager to please my new employers and I worked hard at the hospital in Beacon Hill. Each free day I spent on the South Side and I became good friends with the Natives there. They showed me the ropes: how to make ends meet and where I could get cheaper clothes and how to bargain shop.

Eventually, my pregnancy became noticeable, but I tried for a long time to hide my condition in loose clothes. I didn't want anybody telling me what to do, and I was determined to work as long as I could. Just around the time that I was thinking I would have to give up my job, I had an idea: I could make money baby-sitting for my own people.

Sure enough, I found work looking after a little boy who belonged to a couple I had met my first day in Boston. They gave me room and board in exchange for my services. My room was smaller than the one I had been used to in the hospital, but their five-year-old was easy to look after.

As I came closer to the end of my pregnancy, the couple I was working for asked if they could adopt my baby. I began to think that this would be a good idea; I doubted whether I would be able to look after a child. My friends pointed out to me that I had to work and survive on my own, and that I had no decent place to take care of a baby. As I waited for my child to be born, I became more and more scared about all these things.

My baby was finally born at the Boston City Hospital on August 11, 1951. She was perfect. I examined her all over — she was so small and pretty. I cannot give her away, I thought. I love her. She's mine, she's mine.

Though I was still scared, I couldn't agree to the adoption of my little girl, even after she was named Phyllis Rose by the couple I had been working for. I just did not want to part with her.

Instead, I found an apartment where the landlady offered to care for Phyllis while I worked. Shortly after that, I came home one day to find that the baby would not take her bottle. I took her to the doctor. "The baby's windpipe is narrow," he said. "How do you feed her from a bottle?" There seemed to be no option except to care for Phyllis myself and breast-feed her.

From that time on, everything was fine. I applied for Mothers Allowance to look after my own child and I took good care of her and showered her with love. All my life, with all my children, I have tried my best to give them the love I would have liked for myself.

■ ■ ■

In Boston, even after Phyllis was born, I was still making some mistakes, searching for the person to spend my life with. I met a Native man, Leo, and thought I was in love with him until I found out that he was going around with another girl at the same time as he was going with me. We parted ways, but not before I became pregnant. A little boy, Robert — Bobby, as I called him — was born one year after Phyllis. I looked after my two children by myself, still hoping that someday I would meet an individual who would feel the same way about me as I thought I felt each time I fell in love. After a while, I met another Mi'kmaq, Lawrence Francis. He was an easy-going person — a widower, with children of his own, from Pictou Landing in Cape Breton. We became engaged in 1953.

That year, Phyllis was two and Bobby was one. I decided that they were old enough to leave with a sitter again. Just around the time I was planning to look for work outside the home, I had an unexpected visitor — a man who came knocking at my door, asking for his cousins. He was tall and handsome and he talked in English to me and stared into my eyes intently. We only spoke briefly, and I remember thinking that he looked like he might be Italian. He told me that he was living in Portland, Maine but that his family was from Eskasoni, Cape Breton. I had heard the name of the place but had never been there. What a strange name, I thought. I directed the stranger to where his cousins lived with their wives, explaining that the men were at work but would be home soon. I was so flustered, though, that I forgot to ask who he was. After he was gone, it registered with me that the young man must be *Lnu* (Native) because his two cousins were Native. My heart was thumping wildly.

That evening, as I sat in a restaurant talking Indian with Lawrence Francis, I was introduced to the stranger again. I learned that his name was Frank Joe and that he was twenty-four years old. His gaze was still intent, and he didn't seem to care that I was with another man — instead, he openly flirted with me. I disliked his smug attitude.

After Frank Joe left us, I noticed that I had lost my keys, which had been sitting on the table. I was upset and petrified of having to wake my landlady to get into my apartment. My fears came true in a way I did not expect. When I rang the apartment building doorbell later on, my landlady was fit to be tied: Not only had I woken her up, we found the young stranger from Portland, Maine, standing outside my door. My landlady did not approve of male visitors. "Go away!" I hollered at Frank Joe, not thinking to ask how he had got into the building. "You just got me into trouble!" I wanted to wring his neck.

The rest of that week I found it difficult to go anywhere as I still could not find my keys. Frank Joe had them, but I did not know that yet. Finally, a letter arrived from Portland. My keys were in the envelope, along with an apology and a request to visit me.

Frank arrived for his visit on a Sunday, just as I was putting Phyllis into a little yellow dress and getting ready to leave the house. "May I come in?" he asked. He was looking at me intently again, but he was talking in a very gentle, very nice voice. Later, he told me that that was the moment when he said to himself, "I'm going to marry that woman."

"My landlady is fussy about men visiting," I said. I left the door of my apartment open for her benefit and we made polite conversation. Mostly, we spoke about my brother Matt, whom he knew; I also knew Frank's sister, Theresa, from residential school. We had not been there at the same time, but I knew of her. We spoke in English the whole time; I thought Frank preferred conversing in that language. Finally, he said, "*Siknoqkwa tasi* (I am tired of hearing myself)," and asked if I would speak Mi'kmaq instead of English with him. Mi'kmaq was our common voice from then on.

On his third visit, Frank asked me to marry him.

"Why all the rush?" I wondered. We were sitting in a restaurant at the time, talking.

"I got a job," he replied. "When I came to visit you the last time, I applied at the Massachusetts General Hospital and went for an interview." He showed me his ID from the hospital; I still have that ID today. "I'm in a secure job," he told me, "and we can get married right away."

"What will I do with the guy I've promised to marry?" I asked him. Lawrence was away at the time — he had gone home to Canada to attend the funeral of his father. I did not know yet that Frank, too, was already engaged to someone else: a non-Native woman — a nurse.

Frank Joe looked into my eyes and said, "You'll do the same thing I will do to my girl back home — write a 'Dear John' letter."

After this proposal, I went to see a good friend of mine, Annie Johnson. She's still a good friend of mine today. "Annie," I said, "I've got a big problem and I've got to share it with someone." I told her that I was engaged to one man, but that another had asked me to marry him. "Which one should I marry?"

The way she put it to me was like this: "The first man is a nice, gentle, good-natured guy — very nice, very kind, but not ambitious. The second one, he's got a family that is blunt. They're a swearing, rough kind of family. The mother is like a war-horse. But he's ambitious."

Frank and I wrote our letters home (I was too cowardly to send the letter directly to Lawrence, so I sent it to his sister) and we got married not long after that, on January 15, 1954.

■ ■ ■

Frank Joe was a good man. I loved him so deeply — he was the first man after my dad and my brothers whom I loved that much. I am not sorry to have chosen him, but there were times in our life together that were very, very hard. Before we married, and early on, he was so dear and so nice to me. But, later, there were some tough years. The storybook union I had hoped for faded from my mind as time wore on, but I did the best I could and always hoped for a better tomorrow. The eight children I had with my husband gave me courage.

I believed in being faithful to one man, so I was always faithful to Frank. And I wanted to prove to myself that I could be a good mother and wife, so I had a glass of beer the day before we got married and never touched liquor again. I put down my cigarettes and never touched them again. I tried to prove all this to Frank, too — but for a long time he mistrusted me and, after awhile, he beat me. I was a battered woman for many years.

The way I look at it, Frank was in a difficult situation, too. His father had died when Frank was seven, so he had only one parent. His mother sent two of her four children — including Frank — to the residential school, and for him this was a very negative experience. He was very bright, but he had to stop going to school when he was thirteen years old, in Grade Nine. His mother made him quit school and work for wood and water. His life had been hard like mine, except that he had less opportunity to educate himself. He had worked in Sydney from the time he was thirteen, and brought food home to his mother and little brothers and sisters. In the back of his mind, he always thought that he had not achieved his full potential. So, from the time we were first married, I built up that man's ego and I built up his spirit. Whatever Frank wanted to do, I encouraged him in it.

We had many hardships and I put up with a lot of things over the years, always hoping for a better tomorrow. Perhaps I thought that I had had difficult experiences when I was little — but I had hard times again when I was married.

> Two roads we go, there's no one else around
> Two roads we travel, 'til happiness we find.
> And when we find it, we try with all our heart
> To make the best of everything.
> Two roads we try, to win the game.

■ ■ ■

At first, being married was like playing house. Oh, we were so happy! Frank worked all day as an operating room technician at the Massachusetts General Hospital. He would come home and read the paper, and then we would eat our meal together, which I tried to cook the way he liked. Little Phyllis loved her new dad, and he would laugh at her ways. I remember one time when Phyllis was in the living room with Frank and she lost her bottle. Frank was reading the newspaper, while I was in the tiny kitchen making supper. Finally, Frank hollered out to me, "Rita! Come help Phyllis. She's looking for something."

When I came, he asked her, "What are you looking for, Phyllis?" And she said, "I'm looking for my bolloo!" We laughed so hard — she was two years old and very serious, looking everywhere for her bottle. Phyllis is over forty now and I still tease her sometimes about looking for her "bolloo."

Our newlywed state was nice while it lasted. There was hardship, though. We had to concentrate on our budget, to make sure we could pay for everything and buy what we needed. After a little while, I realized that one of Frank's cousins would wait for Frank on payday. When Frank got off the bus after work, there was the cousin. They would go off together and, by the time I got hold of him, half of Frank's salary would be gone and he'd be stone drunk. That was the hard part.

Also, Frank did not want me to keep Bobby. I loved my son, but I also loved Frank blindly. I did what he asked me to do: I took Bobby to my sister Annabel, who found a good home for him with a couple in Eskasoni. This couple, John and Mary Agnes Marshall, loved my son like he was their own. He grew into a nice-looking boy, but died unexpectedly several years later, when he was still young. When he died, I cried all the more for not knowing him all those years; the empty feeling I experienced inside me cannot be described. John and Mary Agnes loved Bobby — that is all I hang onto.

> A little toddler ran across my path
> On his way back, I reached out my hand
> To hug and keep him warm.
> The stretch of hand produced air
> And he ran away to hide behind a crib.
> Like all little boys in mischief his eyes dared,
> But with no fear from him or me
> Both of us seemed to care.
>
> Once in a while he comes to his former home
> The toddler boy from another age
> Now a shadow.

A few months after being married, I was pregnant again. One day just after our little girl, Evelyn — whom we nicknamed Step — was born, Frank came home from work and announced, "We're going home to Canada." Without my knowledge, Frank had applied for a job as an orderly at the Victoria General Hospital in Halifax. Now, that job was waiting for him. I packed up our belongings, my heart in a turmoil. I loved Frank so much that I jumped to do whatever he wanted me to do. He told me he had realized that the United States was not the place for us to be, because the salary he earned in an American hospital was one-half of what he could earn in Canada. I hoped that he was right, and that our future would be better back in Halifax.

■ ■ ■

Step was about ten days old when we traveled to Halifax on the train. We settled down in an apartment on Victoria Road. It had been difficult to find the apartment, and when we did, the conditions were poor for what we had to pay. Frank's job put food on the table, but didn't leave much extra money. He worked very hard, his time with us unpredictable.

My sister-in-law, Theresa, also lived in Halifax. She was married to a petty officer in the Navy and had a better life than we did. She knew how poor we were. We had so little: just a small hot plate, and I had to carry our drinking water from a tap in the bathroom upstairs.

I remember Theresa's kindness when our next child — a little boy, Francis, whom we called Junior — was born in September 1955. Frank was away in Maine at the time, and he kissed the phone when he called the hospital and learned that he had a son.

> I am tired in early evening
> I lay on the couch relaxing in a half-doze.
> This is the seventh month of pregnancy.
> A spirit monk is bending over my stomach
> Looking, as if with concern;
> I wish him away.
> A short time later I go to hospital
> Today I have a strapping boy
> That a monk came to see one day.

I had Phyllis' old clothes and Step's old clothes, but I didn't have diapers for Junior. Theresa came by with a big flannelette blanket, all worn smooth, and said, "You can cut that up into diapers." The blanket sure made handy diapers, but they were funny-looking: I had no needle and thread to sew the hem, so they became raggedy when I hung them on the line to dry!

I also remember Christmas Eve that year, when Junior was only three months old. Frank had to work all that day and the next. We had nothing good to eat and there were no toys for the children — no little treats or anything. I remember looking out the window after Frank had gone off to work, and I could see the police station across the street and all the lights on the sidewalk and the people shopping, carrying their parcels. Santa Claus was standing on the opposite corner. And I remember feeling envy — there was nothing for us, not even dinner.

The next day, Christmas Day, there was a knock on the door in the afternoon. I opened the door and standing there was an Indian man. I didn't recognize him. "Are you Rita — Rita Joe?" he asked.

"Yeah," I said, and he handed me a shoe box. "Your sister-in-law sent this for your dinner," he told me and then he left.

I opened the shoe box. My sister-in-law had lined the box with foil and plastic, and inside there were potatoes, corn, chicken — even cake. Everything was right there in that shoe box. Of course, I served it right away to Phyllis, who was running around the apartment, and Step, who was two. Then I ate what was left over. When Frank came home, I told him about his sister. To this day, I thank that woman.

Despite hardship, we made sure the children always had enough to eat and drink. Frank would bring home little containers of milk from work and there was a store nearby where I would hand the lady at the counter a quarter and she would give me a great big bag of broken cookies. I guess she knew I was strapped for money, so she would pack the bag full. I would go to that store whenever I could afford the quarter. There was also a meat store across the road from us where I could get ends of meat — ends of bologna, ends of bacon and ham. I would go shopping, and I'd have Phyllis and Step walking along with me — Step was only barely walking — and I'd be carrying Junior. I would ask for twenty-five cents worth of meat, please. And the guy at the counter, I guess he knew we were poor too. He would pack my bag with the ends of meat. That's how we survived in Halifax.

By now, Frank and I had had two children together and I felt that they cemented our relationship; my love for my husband was enough to make me continue to overlook any unpleasant quarrels we might have.

■ ■ ■

In 1956, I had a miscarriage and then another little boy, Clifford. That was a hard time. We were barely surviving. Frank talked it over with me, and we decided to put Phyllis, who was five, into the Shubenacadie Indian Residential School for a little while. We knew she would get an education there, and would be cared for until we were better off. A little while after that, we also decided to move the family away from Halifax — this time, to live with Frank's mother in Frank's home reserve of Eskasoni, Cape Breton. Step would be school age soon, and we thought it was better for her to go to school there than in Halifax. We considered Halifax to be dangerous — we always locked our door while we lived there. In Eskasoni we didn't lock doors, and we still don't.

In the fall of 1956, I travelled to Eskasoni with Step, Junior and Clifford while Frank stayed in Halifax to work. He promised to send me money and planned to come and visit us once a month on the reserve. Phyllis we kept in the residential school until we could get a home of our own; she was receiving good care and it was hard enough to be moving into Frank's mother's house with three small children. Later, when we were settled, we would keep her home for good. Sometimes, even today, Phyllis and I talk about that time; she understands the hardship we were having and says her years at the residential school were not that bad.

I remember arriving in Eskasoni for the first time. I got off the train very early in the morning with my small children, the baby in my arms. A man — a non-Native person — got off with us. He had been drinking on the train. By then, I hated drinking. This man was from Christmas Island, which is close to Eskasoni, and while we were still on the train he came over to where I was sitting and said, "You getting off at Christmas Island, huh?" I answered yes, and he said, "Then you have to drive over to Eskasoni. I'll get off with you."

"Somebody will meet me," I told him. I was thinking to myself, "Boy, I really don't want to get off with you." But I came to depend upon that man later.

When we got off the train, it was five in the morning. It was storming and waves of rain were pelting the old station. We went into the station and found that there was no fire in the old, pot-bellied stove. I had my little ones huddled close to me, under my coat. The man from the train was still half-cut but he began looking for wood. Everything he found was wet. Finally, he found a ragged old rotten coat and he put it in the stove along with some wood. Then he took one of the station's kerosene lamps and emptied the kerosene on top of the wood and lit the stove. Pretty soon, he had a good fire going. Oh, I appreciated that. The man looked at me and said, "You weren't speaking to me on the train, but you're friends with me now, I guess!"

I had to say "yes" to this, but I also thanked the man for what he had done and he stayed with us and kept the fire going until someone came and picked me up.

As it turned out, my mother-in-law had hired somebody to drive me to Eskasoni in a truck. We were driving along and this fellow asked me, in Mi'kmaq, "So, how do you like it here?"

I said, "Oh, it looks okay." I didn't really know how to answer. I hadn't arrived at the reserve yet and I had never been to Eskasoni before. Just as I was trying to think of something else to say, a bunch of noisy crows flew by. So I said, "Everything's okay except those crows!" I used the Mi'kmaq word for "crow."

The driver began to laugh. What is so funny? I wondered. I didn't say anything else, I just sat there holding my children and thinking that maybe I had said something wrong in Mi'kmaq. When we arrived at my mother-in-law's house, the man told my mother-in-law what I had said and they both laughed. We went into the house and my mother-in-law told the other family members, "When we asked her how she liked the place, she said she liked it okay except for the crows!" Finally, after everyone finished laughing, she explained that the people on the reserve all had clan names, although the names were mostly humorous and used as a joke. The man who had driven me onto the reserve belonged to a clan known as the Crows.

> A winding bay embraces the land
> With spirited hills a protection.
> The giving seas and the prize
> My hunger ease, lifegiving.
>
> My joy is here on the reservation
> Where my part remains true.
> And the mingling of hearts
> To perception role, unafraid.
>
> We must move like the rivers
> Moving and protesting.
> The undertaking of our heritage is
> Our history we continue.

■ ■ ■

Living on the reservation was different from living in Halifax. As in all Native communities, the people helped each other. There are some people in Eskasoni who have helped me in more ways than I can say. There is a friendly atmosphere among my people that I have always known and felt — we share stories, problems, caring for our babies, recipes for Native herbal medicines — and hardship sometimes seems less hard because we can talk about it with each other. The soupbone making the rounds is our favourite joke. I have been sharing problems and jokes with friends, especially other women on the reservation, since I arrived in Eskasoni in 1956. The friends I made then are still my friends. That is why I like living on a reservation, even today. It is like living with an extended family.

I had hard times at first, though. It was difficult to live in my mother-in-law's home. My mother-in-law was an ambitious, hardworking woman. At the crack of daylight she would get up and start work. We had no electric stove — just a wood stove — and she would haul in the wood for the day and cook. The house was always clean, and everything was always done by noon.

My mother-in-law was the boss in her family. Whatever she said was the law. As a young woman, she had been very beautiful — like a movie star, slim and pretty. She was still beautiful when I lived with her. She had married twice for necessity, but never for love. The first man she had married was Frank's father, when she was eighteen and he was forty-two. She had four children by him. She became a widow when Frank was seven, and later she had married again. Her life had been hard, and when I first went to live with her I realized that all those things my friend Annie in Boston had told me were true. All the members of her family were blunt. I heard lots of "You fucking whore," and that kind of talk.

The rest of the family were great drinkers and smokers, but I was not. All I wanted to do was look after my children and keep the house in order. I washed clothes and hauled water and brought the wood in. Everything that you could possibly do, I did it just so. I even tried to make baskets. My mother-in-law would make fun of my basket-making; I had never learned how to make baskets properly and had to take lessons from her.

But I said to myself, "I'm going to earn her respect. And all these people who are putting me down — I'm going to earn their respect too." And I did. It took me years and years, but no matter how angry or mean my mother-in-law was with me, I returned her words with kindness. In the end, I loved that old lady so much, and she loved me. But she didn't tell me that she loved me for a long while, and meanwhile I found living in her house very, very hard.

> The art forms in mind
> The production originates.
> Imagination plays the tune
> Where creation settles.

If the bloom is to succeed
The flower must be in wonder.
For the viewer eyes the end transformation
Of the task in mind
The basketmaker promises.

■ ■ ■

On one of Frank's visits home, I found a woman's picture in his wallet. "Who's this?" I asked him.

"Oh," he said. "That's no one. It doesn't mean anything." But the picture broke my heart and I tore it to pieces. Once I was in Frank's arms I felt secure again — the woman really did not mean anything, I told myself. I believed my husband's every word. I had to believe him. All my life I had looked for love, and I had been disappointed so many times by other people. This man who had married me, who had given me his name — I had to believe what he told me. When Frank went back to Halifax, the torn picture faded from my mind. I was busy with my young children and with trying to live in my mother-in-law's house. The children loved their grandmother, but they were also wary of her cross tongue.

The time finally came when I could not take living in that house anymore. In November 1956, Clifford died. He was only three months old. I remember he had black hair, a very light complexion and a dimple on his chin — he was altogether a beautiful baby. I often think of him and wonder what he would look like today. After he died I was so unhappy, and, more than ever, I wanted to live in my own place and to ration the money Frank sent me myself. One winter day, I bundled up Step and Junior and walked the mile to Chief Wilfred Prosper's house. I begged him to help me. "I will stay anywhere as long as I can be with my children and not depend on anyone," I told him. "Please. Any house, a room, somebody's basement — I don't care."

"It's impossible," he replied sadly. "There are no spare houses in the community, and there are other, homeless people."

I remember there were big snowflakes falling as I pulled my children home in the sled, downhearted and wondering what would become of us. Frank wasn't sending us as much money as he had promised. When this happened, his family gave me a hard time. They were providing for fourteen people in that house.

When I arrived, my mother-in-law happened to be home and she sized up my situation. "I was playing cards with a woman today," she told me. "She's a widow who has people living in her house because she can't live there herself. They're not taking very good care of it, so she's looking for someone else to take it over."

I jumped up and said, "I'll scrub it from top to bottom and keep it clean and take good care of it!" Right away, I went to see the woman who owned the place, and she agreed that I could move in.

When I began living in the widow's house, the first thing I did was scrub and scrub. Oh, the place was a mess when I first went in there. The people who had lived there before were just teenagers — maybe twelve or fourteen years old — and they didn't know how to take care of it. The stuff I had to lug out of that house! There was no bathroom, so you can imagine what I had to lug out, overflowing. Then I had to scrub what mess was left. But I did scrub, until the place was spotless. The floors were shining and the walls were whitened brightness. I sectioned off one area where the stove was, and that's where we lived. My double bed was at one end of the area, and there was a little table for eating and a shelf and a kerosene lamp. My mother-in-law got hold of a barrel that had been full of corned beef, scrubbed it clean and ordered one of her sons to fill it with water each day, so that I would not have to lug water from the well down the road. I only had the one lamp for light, and wood and coal for heat, but I was happy to be living alone with my small children. I spent my time making quilts and cleaning everything in sight. At last, my children could run around and yell to their hearts' content.

My happiness ended all of a sudden one morning, when I woke up and had difficulty lifting my head from my pillow. I went to see a doctor, and right away he checked me into the hospital. "I'm just amazed you're standing on your feet, your blood pressure is so high," he said. In the hospital, I was questioned about my living conditions, my eating habits and the fluids I was drinking. Finally, I mentioned the barrel outside our door that held our water. "What barrel?" asked the doctor.

"Well," I said, "the barrel that my mother-in-law got for me from the store."

"What used to be in that barrel?" asked the doctor. When I answered "corned beef," he told me that we'd found the culprit: Saline-tainted water had almost killed me before I even suspected anything was wrong.

I was in the hospital for five or six days. Over the weekend, Frank came home for a visit. He had never been happy about me moving out of his mother's house. "Why did you move out?' he demanded now. Oh, he was angry. I tried to explain how impossible it had been to live there, but he didn't understand.

Finally, my blood pressure went back to normal and I was able to go home. Frank took me to his mother's house at first, but soon he returned to Halifax and I moved into the widow's house again. It was the only way I could have peace of mind. The children were happy and we fell back into our routine, with Frank visiting from Halifax whenever he could. We enjoyed our home and I was glad to be able to bring up my children my own way. The in-laws, now at a distance, were good to me.

All this time, I worked hard on my relationship with my mother-in-law. I wanted her to love me, because, for so long, I had not had a mother. In many ways, she tried to show me her love, but it was not easy for her to express affection and she was always gruff. She had rough words — but good ones — for my husband, too. She would tell me, "You have to put your foot down once in awhile. You're a doormat, but you don't want to be a doormat all your life." Because she had married for necessity, she could not always understand how I felt about my husband, even though he was her own son.

I loved Frank Joe so much, I continued to ignore his drinking and womanizing. Frank was a good, good man, but for a long time he was torn. He wanted to have his own life — a better life. He had had such high hopes for himself. When we married and had children, one after the other, he felt like he couldn't realize his ambition. The more he thought this, the more I tried to support him in whatever he did. I continued to build him up.

Still, the longer we lived apart, the greater Frank's mistrust of me grew. I think that when men fool around themselves, they think you're doing it too — even if you're not. And, after awhile, you have fights. The more I said, "I'm not with anybody," the more angry he got. He began to beat me.

I hid the bruises. If I went to church and had a bruise, I would wear a kerchief or long-sleeved blouses. If I had a black eye, I'd wear sunglasses. But people in the community were not stupid; they knew what was going on. I made excuses and always, always expressed my love for my husband.

> Two roads we go, there's no one else around
> Two roads we travel, the most we look to find.
> And sometimes nowhere, the answer we can't find.
> And it hurts to lose on everything,
> The road not always there to win.

■ ■ ■

Less than a year after we moved to Eskasoni, I was pregnant again. Frank decided that it was time to live with us. He found another job, as a nursing assistant at a hospital in Sydney, Nova Scotia. We packed up and moved to Membertou Reservation, outside of Sydney, and entered into the familiar routine: the barely existing paycheque, and me bargain hunting for clothes, food or whatever else we needed. I had learned long ago how to budget on small amounts of money. We called it "ro'kewte'likan" — "crooked buying." As long as I had flour and yeast, and lots of wood, my house would smell of home baking. I always managed to get a lot of potatoes, onions and bean pork for "hash-a-wey," which was sliced potatoes cooked with the bean pork and onions and simmered to make it tasty. I made sure our children ate good meals; I did not want them to know the hunger I had known.

Today, my children remember that there was always lots of food in our home. Little Junior would come home with his friends and say, "See! I told you my mother would have home-baked bread!"

Working at the St. Rita Hospital in Sydney was good for my husband. He had a circle of friends among the non-Natives in the area, and soon everybody in the community of Membertou Reservation became friends with us too. Frank loved sports and took Junior along to his ball games on the reservation field.

Our life in the community was good, if full of the usual ups and downs. I remember one day, when my husband was at work and the children were playing outside. I looked out my window, as I did habitually when the children were small, and noticed that Junior was nowhere in sight. I became frantic. A while back, a small child had disappeared and was never found. I had the community in an uproar, looking everywhere for my little boy. We even checked the little stream behind my house. As all this was happening, a truck pulled into the driveway and my son jumped out, full of stories about his time with his "Uncle Wallace." Wallace was my favourite cousin — he was the one I had played with when we were both small — but I yelled at him that day for taking my child without permission. Wallace's face fell and he apologized. "I love the little guy and I just wanted to take him for a ride," he explained. I was appalled by the idea of a child of mine being taken anywhere without my permission. I knew Wallace was a good man, but I made sure he asked before taking Junior anywhere again.

While I was in Membertou, I started making crafts. The other women in the community encouraged my creative endeavours, but I still couldn't make anything worth selling and I needed money. One of the women suggested that I could work in the non-Native houses in Sydney, cleaning; so this is what I did.

Each morning, I would start out early — as soon as the baby-sitter arrived — and catch the bus to town, along with many other women from the reservation. I was glad to earn the five dollars an all-day cleaning paid. I would wash floors and walls, and even climb onto wobbly stepladders to reach high ceilings. I would work all day and then hurry home to have supper on before my husband arrived from work. I did not want Frank to forbid me my freedom to be away from the house and earn money.

My freedom did come to an end one day, though. All that day, as I worked at one of my house cleaning jobs, I felt uncomfortable with a headache and sore back. At four o'clock, the lady of the house told me to come down and eat a lunch she had prepared. I remember it was milk, cake and strawberries. "You did a good job," she told me, "removing that furniture and washing the walls." I thanked her for the compliment and left soon after. My head and back were still bothering me as I hurried to the corner store to buy milk and a few other things I needed. I was headed for the aisle where I knew there was milk when the world went black.

The next thing I remember was a voice saying, "Rita. Rita. What's wrong?"

I had fallen on the floor, and the store clerks had assumed I was drunk. An Indian woman, Isobel, had happened to walk by on her way home from work; the store clerks called her in. When Isobel saw me lying on the floor, she realized something was wrong. She knew who I was; the assumption that I was drunk did not sound right to her. She bent over me and called my name.

I told Isobel to call an ambulance. She rushed over to the telephone and the manager of the store brought me a chair and water. "Sit here and drink this," he told me.

I knew by then that I was hemorrhaging. "Stupid men," I thought to myself. "They never understand women's problems." A crowd of people had gathered to watch; I saw an old lady standing there looking at me. I couldn't tell what had happened to Isobel, so I called the old lady over, and she bent down to listen to me. "Please call an ambulance," I said. "I'm hemorrhaging." That lady moved so fast to do what I asked that the ambulance came almost immediately. I was rushed to the hospital.

Frank was told that I was at St. Rita's Hospital, and he quickly came to my side. He had imagined that I was in a car accident. Now, my world of earning a few bucks came to a halt. "Stay home and mind the children," my husband said.

■ ■ ■

Another little boy, Basil, was born to Frank and me in August 1957. Soon after this, we returned to Eskasoni to be closer to Frank's family. Frank hitchhiked back and forth to work in Sydney each day; my world became the children and Frank.

By this time, we had four children. I loved all of them. From the time they were small, I tried to communicate and listen to them. I talked to them like they were adults. When you are a child, you look up to adults. I have fond memories of people who were kind to me and I also have bad memories of people who were unkind. So I tried to be kind and cheerful with my children and not frighten them with scolding or harshness.

They were growing into beautiful people, each with a distinct identity. Phyllis, who came home from the Shubenacadie school on holidays, was lovely and shy, and Step was always tagging along with her; Junior was not quite school age and took after me and my father's side of the family, with light skin and curly light hair. When my mother-in-law first saw Junior she said to me, "We have a stranger here!" because he was so blond when he was small. I never said anything, but I knew in my heart that my ancestry was showing itself. Later, Junior became darker and today that particular son is the spitting image of his father. Our other little fellow, Basil, was as dark as Frank from the day he was born and always getting into some mischief. I called Basil and Junior "night and day." Once, when Basil was sitting by the side of the road playing with his little cars in the mud, my mother-in-law told me to dress him in brighter colours. "Nobody can see Basil in dark clothes," she said. "He's the same colour as the mud." Basil laughs at this story today.

While my children were growing up, I shared many problems and stories with friends in the community. I remember one occasion in 1960, when I became ill with bleeding ulcers. It had never occurred to me that I might be ill, until one day I took my two small sons for their noon nap upstairs and lay beside them singing and talking in a soothing voice until they were asleep.

While lying on the bed, I felt nauseous, so I went downstairs and began to vomit blood. I told one of the older children to fetch a neighbour, and the neighbour took me to the hospital. I was there for ten days. The day I came home, an old friend, Mrs. Ma'n Julian, brought me a gallon bottle and set it on the table. "You drink this every day," she said.

"What is it?" I asked.

"Never you mind what the hell it is!" she said. "Just drink it."

So I drank it every day and very soon I was doing hand-springs. The gallon bottle was full of a herbal medicine my friend had prepared when she heard I was coming home. I could fill a book with stories like that, about the kindness of friends from day to day.

I remember another incident a few years later, when I was awakened by Frank early one morning. I was needed by a friend, Francis (Francho) Stevens. She was going to have a baby and had asked me to help her get ready for the hospital. She was all alone in her mother's house; her family members were away in Maine, picking blueberries. I brought along a washpan so that Francho could get washed, and she asked me to help her get a suitcase for packing. As I was doing this, she called out, "Look!"

I turned around and pretty nearly fainted: The baby was coming. Gently, I coaxed Francho to lie on the sofa, all the while shoving underneath her anything I could get hold of. The baby was guided by my hands, while my eyes were blinded by tears. "Don't you cry!" Francho said.

I was so relieved that the baby was all right, I cried tears of joy. That was a happy day for me; I became one of the baby's godparents. Francho was one of my foster sisters from a home I had stayed in as a child, and she had always been a close friend. She died several years ago, and I miss her. Her child, Kimberly Stevens, is a grown woman today.

I like to think of our native life,
Curious, free;
And look at the stars
Sending icy messages.
My eyes see the cold face of the moon
Cast his net over the bay.

It seems
We are like the moon —
Born,
Grow slowly,
Then fade away, to reappear again
In a never-ending cycle.

All this time, my husband worked hard, lived hard, and struggled to master our lot in life. I knew he felt like he was going nowhere and that our difficult life bothered him. But he tried his best — oh, he was such a hardworking man. I never saw anyone work as hard as Frank did. I remember when they were putting in a water line here in the community, and the men got paid forty dollars for each deep, six-foot-long trench they could dig in a day. It was bad enough to dig a trench, but Frank had to dig two so that he could earn eighty dollars a day. From dawn till dark, and sometimes even after dark, he'd work so that he could earn those eighty dollars. The trenches would be measured and the men would be paid at the end of the week — they were allowed to work five or six days a week. And at the end of the week Frank was able to buy us things — blankets, pots, pans. I still have those pots and pans.

At home, I continued to build up Frank's ego. Everything he did I praised, and everything I did was to please him and the children. The problem in all this was Frank's drinking. His frustration became evident as he drank, and the beatings he gave me became a more frequent part of my life. Our children saw it all. They could not prevent it, but their love for me was what held me together.

"*Yi-ya* (Does it hurt), Mom?" they would ask, touching my bruises. I often cried into their hair and wiped my tears on their clothes. When I hugged my children, I tried to find comfort in their love for the pain consuming my soul at that moment.

> The battered women in all walks of life are there
> The ill-treatment we undergo, psyches us out
> Jumping to do our duties, reasoning love
> Obeying blindly, until it is too much to bear.
> At first I hid my hurt in long-sleeved blouses
> The ache in my heart driving lonely thoughts inward
> Believing the love words, dependant
> Our children there looking up to me
> Wanting to believe so very much, the love reward.
> This went on for years at first.
> Most of the time we were compatible, friendly
> But liquor always got its way.

■ ■ ■

My seventh child, Bernadette Isobel, was born to us on April 7, 1959. I remember her curly black hair and large, expressive eyes so well. This baby was joined in one year — on April 29, 1960 — by our daughter Frances, and again a few years later by Caroline, a ten-pound beauty born on March 4, 1963. The nurses at St. Rita's hospital in Sydney took her everywhere, showing her off. Because Frank worked there, they knew how much he admired his children.

> She was born to us in early spring.
> A pretty daughter, my heart sang.
> Followed by others, she was unique;
> I could not put my finger on it.
> As time passes the show of senses,
> My longing realized, they became real.
> She is special like all children.
> *Ke'salu'kik* (We love them) *aqq kesaluksi'kik* (and they love us).

It was around this time, when Frank and I had been married for almost ten years, that we finally built our own house in

Eskasoni, and kept Phyllis, who was twelve, home to stay. I remember Frank trying to finish the house the summer before Caroline was born. Oh, that poor guy: He worked on the house all summer, until twelve o'clock at night, every night. I would hear the hammer, and then finally I'd hear it stop and know he was on his way home. He used to get people to help by making a batch of home-brew and offering it to whoever was working with him. The snag was that whenever they finished a part of the house, they'd drink themselves into a state.

I put up with a lot of dehumanizing things in those years, hoping always for a better tomorrow. In the mid-1960s, after the problems with Frank had gone on for several years, I read somewhere that openly talking about battering often creates peer pressure for the abuser to stop. So I began to run away from home for periods of time. I would live with friends and relatives and tell my story to anyone who listened. By that time, my children were older. The youngest were mystified by my absence, but the older ones were eager to look after the little ones so that their mother might somehow resolve this problem.

One person I talked to was my friend Mrs. Margaret Johnson. From time to time over the years, Margaret has come across for me in more ways than I can say. Margaret even tried to talk to Frank herself, as a friend, because her husband John was Frank's cousin. Surprisingly, Frank listened to her.

Another close friend was Anna Jean (Joogie) Doucette. She was a little younger than me but we shared some of the same problems and so we always had a lot to talk about. Often, on her way home from her sister's place, she would stop at my house. I would fold a quilt four ways and put it on the floor so that she could feed one of her babies and hold the other on her lap, and still talk to me. Later, Joogie died of cancer; I loved her like a sister and I miss our talks.

Sometimes, I'd even try to work on the compassion of the women who took my husband. And, once, after I found out that one of his women was from the community, I went out and I smashed every window in our car. It was a good car — not a brand-new car, but a good car. I beat that car to pieces, I was so frustrated. This woman was going with my husband, in front of my face, in front of my children. The people in the community could not understand what I had done: Finally, Rita went beserk, they said. They knew I had been a doormat for many years, but they couldn't understand what I had done because it meant hardship for my family — Frank and I had to pay for that car, and it was difficult.

But I told Frank, "I will do the same thing again if another situation develops. If I smash up a car, the car doesn't cry. I didn't kill anyone, I didn't beat up that woman, I didn't beat up my husband and I didn't hurt anything but that car. It's made of metal. It didn't cry." That was my philosophy.

Frank called me crazy. He said, "You're insane to do that." I knew I was not crazy, but you take that much from anybody and you go off your rocker. For a moment I believed Frank, because I had an uncle who was a very depressed man and had been in the hospital for thirty years. So I told my doctor I needed to see a psychiatrist. We had a long session and then I asked the psychiatrist, "Am I crazy?"

"You're as sane as I am," he said.

"Will you put that on a document, because I want to take it home to my husband," I said. I wanted everyone to know that I was as sane as anybody else.

■ ■ ■

In 1967, I was pregnant with my youngest, Ann. I was still having a hard time, but I did not hide my bruises under long sleeves anymore; I even showed them to my mother-in-law. She would tell me, "I married two men, and neither one of them ever laid a hand on me. No one hurt me." It was a heel print on my breast that was the last straw for her. It drove her wild. She comforted me, finally expressing her love for me.

Just before Ann was born, my mother-in-law took matters into her own hands. I thought she would kill my husband, she hit him so hard with a block of wood. "Don't ever lay a hand on Rita again as long as you live!" she screamed at him.

I had always called my mother-in-law "*Kiju'* (Mother)"; from this time on, the word truly held us together.

After a while I began to search for safety,
In the mind as well as the physical,
With other people
Sharing my story with anyone listening
Especially with other women, searching for outlets
Emphasizing how much love was there
But liquor and mistreatment going together.
Our togetherness unsettled, I began to write.
He made fun, but I built my spirit, using culture.
Today I share my story with you
The building comes down sometimes
But we women, by association,
Always stand together.

Another person I went to for help at this time was Mrs. Jessie Gould, who was an elder in Eskasoni. I visited her one night and poured out my misery. She fixed up the chesterfield for me so that I could sleep there and, after hugs and a soothing talk, told me that we would settle the rest the next day. In the morning she told me to go home and tell my husband that I had told her everything. That is what finally brought the problem to a standstill. Public knowledge usually helps, especially in a small community. I think the elders in a community are the best social intermediaries in any situation. In Native communities, we have total respect for the elders; we listen to their common sense more than we listen to professionals. Mrs. Gould was loved by all of us; we miss her now that she is gone.

After that time, Frank's anger at me and the world was not so great. Little by little, things got better. Later on, Mrs. Gould and Frank became the best of friends — he would take the first catch of eels or trout to her. She appreciated that very much.

Two roads we go, there's no one else around
Two roads we travel, sometimes good and sometimes wrong.
And if we find it, we try with all our heart,
giving happiness to others.
Two roads we tried; we won the game.

■ ■ ■

Before Ann, I had two stillborn children. I was very afraid that this child would be stillborn, too. Five months into my pregnancy, I could feel that things weren't right. I pleaded with the doctor to save my baby. I remember he touched me to reassure me and said, "Don't worry, Rita. We'll do everything we can." He appointed two specialists to look after me.

When I was just five and a half months pregnant, I was put into hospital. The doctors were trying to keep my blood pressure down and create an environment with no trauma. At six months and two weeks, they said, "We have to remove the baby now." So I was cut open and Ann was born on October 12, 1967. She was only four pounds — so tiny — and she had to stay in an incubator. But I was so happy to have her. Oh, I was happy. She was my last child.

About a year-and-a-half later, I had a hysterectomy. I was still in my thirties, but I was having a hard time with bleeding, miscarriages and stillborn children. There came a time when the doctor said to me, "If you want to live for the other children, then you must have a hysterectomy."

"Yes!" I said. "Of course I want to live." I knew what it was like to be without a mother, and I didn't want that for my children. I went to see a priest and told him about this choice. "You have to make up your own mind. I cannot tell you what to do," he said. "Do what your heart tells you."

My heart told me that I should be with the children I had. Excuse me, God, I said, I do not want to die like my mother. I have to do it this way.

> This is my life
> The soles of my feet touch
> The fallen brown leaves.
> My soul in expectation
> of the Great Brave.
>
> I am his Indian
> And my native song
> Echoes through the hills.

· · ·

When I was in my thirties, I began to write. The writing was like therapy for me. It addressed my own situation, past and present; it also addressed the situation of my children and my people.

It began when my older children, bringing their homework to me, would point out certain things they did not like. At first, I would say, "Well, for school you have to write it as it says in your book — but we did not do what it says there." I would try to explain that the negative stereotypes were just copied and re-copied in the books, and that our history had not been written by our own people. I had begun explaining this a long time earlier, when our children were very small — but still, when you're young, you accept what is put in front of you.

It was when some of my children were in their teens that the negative stereotypes really began to show up in the history and science books they studied and in the movies they watched. They would say, "Look what it says here, Mom." Oh my gosh, the books said negative things. When Step was sixteen and in Grade Eleven, she came home one day wanting to quit school. One of her history teacher's remarks had hurt her terribly. This teacher had said to her, "Since you are a Mi'kmaq Indian, why not tell the class why the Indians did this to us."

So then I told my children, "When you're in the classroom and you hear a discussion about Natives and you know that what people are saying isn't right, don't hesitate to put up your hand and say, 'I'm a Native and this is what I know.'" I told all my children that, and they did it. It was the only way to set the record straight. One of the important things I kept telling them is that we are the ones who know about ourselves. "Don't fear declaring anything," I said, "because you are the ones who know. You might not be an expert, but you do know."

My father, Josie Gould Bernard, holding his first child, my half-brother William. My father's first wife is on the right. Photo from around 1900.

Elizabeth Googoo, my great-grand-mother on my mother's side. Photo taken between 1900 and 1905.

The only known photo of my mother, Annie Googoo Bernard.

Me and my half-brother William around 1980.

My brother Soln at Whycocomagh in the 1970s.

My brother Roddy in the mid-1970s.

My brother Matt from the mid-1960s.

My sister Annabel in the 1970s.

The Shubenacadie Indian Residential School, where I lived from 1944-48.

My husband, Frank Joe, aged 18.

Frank and me on our
wedding day in 1954.

Me aged 26 *(front)*, with cousins Pauline and Wallace Bernard *(seated)* and friends Katy MacEwen and John Paul *(kneeling)*.

My only photo of my mother-in-law *(middle)*, with my sister-in-law Mary Ann *(left)*, brother-in-law George *(right)* and George's wife Anne *(behind him, at right)*.

Our son Junior, aged 3, in 1958, outside our home in Membertou.

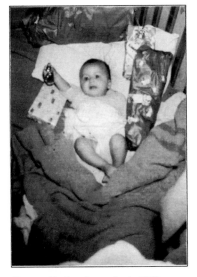

Our son Basil at 4 months, in 1958.

Our children Ann *(front)*, Frances *(left)*, Bernadette *(right)* and Basil *(back)* in the late 1960s.

Junior *(left)* and Frances around 1970.

Our foster child Charlie, me, Junior with T.J. (Frances' son) and our daughters Step and Caroline, in the late 1970s.

Frank and me in 1975.

Frank with Frances' children, T.J. *(left)* and Ann *(right)*, in the early 1980s.

The days have disappeared
and will not return.
Your history tells our children
what you want them to learn.

That the Indian is the violent one
The wars the white man always won.

History records about the men.
Aye! What warriors they were
To deny this never,
For in the earth they lie.

Their bravery, hardships, their deeds
are but a myth, my children read.

What price to pay
They fought for us.
But this
You do not record.

The warriors are past care,
the lies, injustices their fare.

Now, tales are all that are told
Beyond the letters in gold.
Our children learn today
our ancestors were there.

The Great One knows
what price we paid.

It would make me so angry to see movies and realize that the Indian was always the one shooting the others in the back, and to read so often that the Mi'kmaq had never developed their own writing. I would talk to my children and husband about this, and Frank would say, "Well, what are you going to write?"

One day, it just dawned on me that something had to be done. "We have to tell our lot," I said. "We have to be the ones to record our words." Ever since I was little, I have been a reader — I used to read everything I could get my hands on. Sometimes I would see some stories and poems and think, "I could do better than that." So I made the effort and wrote a poem about Eskasoni; I just sat down and wrote it.

When I began to write, if I saw something negative, I put that down; writing about the negative was therapy. But from the time of my first poem, I also looked for beauty — even if it came out of a negative or hated structure.

I remember my first poem — how easy it was to put down on paper. I just looked around me and talked to my people, and I saw the beauty in my land and my culture, as clear as day.

> There are record hops, beaches, community hall and gym
> Folks want entertainment, to each their need.
> Our church with a shrine, we revere.
> The leaders of our people, we respect.
> Our land is here, as far as one sees
> In Eskasoni, near mountains, waters and trees.
>
> For instance, there is Eskasoni Women's Auxiliary
> Our greatest wish is that it succeed.
> The trades we know are a way of release
> To offer our country our achievements.
> If you pass by on your way please
> Come see Eskasoni, near mountains, waters and trees.
>
> Throughout the year, the hills are a view
> Especially in October, like painted pyramids.
> Through the year we hunt and fish
> Depending on resources, that spell Indian,
> Our land always gave, we remember
> In Eskasoni, near mountains, waters and trees.
>
> In the morning we awaken to the sounds outside
> Seeing the beauty of water and the rising tide.
> Listening to old folks telling stories
> Of long ago, when the earth was young.
> Their deeds woven into history
> In Eskasoni, near mountains waters and trees.

SONG OF MY TALK

(1969 — 1989)

EPIT

Supposing you were I and I were you:
You gave, I received
You would think in terms of love
Giving without thought of payment
The words of a culture
To spread and mend

Supposing I were you
And received without question
The words of a culture
Spreading news like yours

With so little, we share
But not so much of my life do you bear
Let us trade places just this once
And you listen while I go on about my culture
Important just like yours
But almost dead.

By the late sixties and into the seventies, all my children except the very youngest were in junior high school and high school. More and more, they experienced immersion into an alien nation. This immersion created some problems.

I remember one incident that was brought to our attention: One of our daughters refused to take off her coat in school. My husband was a Councillor on the reserve at that time and he went to see the principal. He asked if our daughter's work was okay.

"Oh, her work is okay," said the principal.

"Why the big issue about her coat, then?" my husband replied. When he said this, I thought he was ten feet tall.

Another incident occurred when two girls got into a fist fight at school. The non-Native girl was what we called "*aklasiewto't* (white person beaten)," meaning she made a lot of noise about her injuries but was not hurt badly. Meanwhile, the Native girl hid her twisted ankle. The police were called, along with an ambulance for the non-Native. Our leaders got involved then; my husband told the principal that the police should not have been called. Once again, I thought he was brave to express these feelings out loud.

Me, I kept putting my thoughts and feelings down on paper. Although I told my children to speak up about stereotypes, I also taught them not to make waves unless it was necessary. For a long time, I was afraid to say anything too negative; I did not want to offend leaders and educators. I assumed, deep down, they must know the truth about my people.

> Like lava from the heart
> This wonder grows,
> Why was a tale not told?
> Admiration I know for the deeds of my people —
> Their perceptions.

> I know their wants
> I know their ways
> I know their creeds.

> Their love of customs
> Observance of rules.

> *Aknutm te' sik kejitu*

■ ■ ■

After I wrote my first poem about Eskasoni, I sent it to the local Mi'kmaq newspaper. They printed it, and, oh, I got such feedback — I got letters and fan mail and people wrote to the newspaper and commented on my writing. So I wrote more stories and poems and articles. After awhile, I began to write a monthly column for the *Micmac News*.

Each month, I would collect little incidents and anecdotes. If somebody told me something interesting, I would keep it in my mind and jot it down as soon as I could and store it away. Then, when it was time to write, I would sit down and scribble a page or two. I wrote in pen — I didn't have a typewriter — but I would write as clearly as I could so that the editor could read it.

We named the column "Here and There in Eskasoni." My children knew about my writing and were interested; I greatly appreciated their efforts. I remember Junior, when he was about fifteen, trying to help me in my early snatches of writing. He would tell me about the traditional stories he had learnt; the traditional part of his life has always been important to him.

A lot of the stories were about traditional ways and medicine. I would talk to the elderly people and they would tell me what they knew. Mrs. Annie Cremo was one elder I would often go to for stories and advice, along with her sisters Harriet Denny and Helen Cabot. They would tell me their stories in Mi'kmaq and, because of them, I started to use Native words in my little column every month.

> *Jiktek*
> All is still.
> Silence reigns.
> *Tepknuset*
> The moon
> A month
> *Nemi'k*
> I see.
>
> So long ago.
> *Nmis*
> My sister.
> *Maja'sit*
> She go.
> *Nmis*, my sister
> *Nutaq*, I hear
> *Wena*, who?
> *Nekm*, her, him, them.

So long ago.
Api, a bow
Teken, which?
Ji'nm nemi'k
Man I see.
Kwitn, a canoe
App kinu'tmui, teach me again
Lnui'simk, Indian talk.

So long ago.

I remember one story I wrote was about a Native medicine called "*kikwesu'sk* (muskrat root)." I had heard it was good for colds. I fermented it and used it on myself, and it cured my cold, so I felt like I was an expert on the medicine. I set myself to finding out more about it, but I didn't know its English name. I asked different people — many elderly people — if they knew the name in English, but nobody did. I remember that Lee Cremo, the champion fiddler, came into the room when I was asking people about this, and he told me to just use Mi'kmaq names. So I wrote my column about the medicine and spelled the word the way it sounds in Mi'kmaq.

The medicine works like this: You gather it during the summer and string it up to dry, and when it dries, you grind it and put it in a glass of water with a little honey. Then you drink it, and you sweat out your cold. When I took the medicine myself during a bad cold, I swallowed it just before going to bed. In the night I would wake up and my nightgown would be wet with the sweat. Sometimes I'd have to get up and change into another nightgown.

I explained all this in my column and went on to say that I didn't know the English name of the medicine, but that it sounded like "*kikwesu'sk*." Since "*kikwesu*" means "muskrat," I concluded the medicine must be muskrat root. I got a lot of mail about that column, from Alberta, from PEI, from all across the country. Even non-Natives wrote in, because they were interested in the name of the medicine. It turned out that it was flagroot in English, and a lot of people wrote to tell me that I had mispronounced the Mi'kmaq name.

When my husband saw the feedback, he said, "You'd better make sure you know your facts when you're writing about something."

"Well," I said, "at least I got a lot of feedback." This is what I tried to do with the column — everything that I learned, I would write down and discuss. Many people wrote back to me. It made me feel like I was accomplishing something.

> There are stories told by the elderly
> Of bannock baked in a bed of stone
> Of birchbark fashioned into a pot
> To boil meat and bone
>
> There are tales told
> Of what life was before
> Of wigwam in the wood
> With deerskin for a door
>
> Fishing from canoe
> Hunting in the wild
> Herbs gathered for the sick
> To cure and soothe
>
> Prayers and song
> Memories told to the young
> When all life was *Inua'kis*
>
> It will never be the same again
> Only in our minds and elderly tales

■ ■ ■

There came a time when I stopped writing the column. I stopped because I was arrested, for doing something I never should have done.

Frank was working in Sydney at the time and had been living in town, apart from us, for several months. He was making a lot of money and enjoying himself. He came and asked me for a divorce because he was involved with a woman in town — a non-Native woman.

I was really angry. Ann was still less than a year old. I went after that woman and went into her home and pushed her up against a wall. I said, "I've got a baby and a house full of children, and you would take my husband?"

I shouldn't have done what I did; I knew better and I've always known better.

I was arrested for assault and taken into custody. I was also charged with breaking in, because I had walked right into the woman's home; in a non-Native community that's a break-in. It was the first time I had ever been arrested and I wasn't sure what to do. "I think I'm allowed one call," I said. I called up the Union of Nova Scotia Indians; I thought they might have a lawyer who could help me out. My friend Sarah Denny happened to be at the union office that day. Later she told me about the reaction of the people who were there. It was four o'clock in the afternoon when the call came; nobody in higher authority was still in the office. The four women who did happen to be there all looked at each other; they couldn't believe what they had heard. "*Who* did you say was in jail?" they asked the woman who answered the phone in the office. "You know," she answered. "Rita Joe: Here and There."

Soon, the woman who was the Indian Agent was called in, and she took charge. Three of the women from the office went down to the police station where I was being held. I could see them go up to the police officer, but they couldn't see me because I was behind a partition. I just sat quietly; I could hear them talking about me. "There is no bail," the police officer said, and I thought to myself, "Why is there no bail? I did not commit murder. Are they trying to make me into an example?" After a little while, my friends left. I didn't show that I had seen or heard them.

After that, I was put into the lock-up. I sat there and accepted what I had done, and I felt like I was alone, with no one in the world to turn to. It was just misery. In a little while, I was removed from the first cell and taken to another room where I stayed the night. I could not stop crying. A psychologist — a woman — came, and talked to me, but I kept crying and crying. I felt so awful. My husband did not know that I was in jail, and my children didn't know either. I kept thinking of my children. Ann was just a little baby. I told the psychologist that nothing like this had happened to me before; I explained everything to her. She called my doctor, and a little while later she came back with a pill that relaxed me and helped me to sleep.

The next morning, I got up and got dressed and waited to be taken to my arraignment. That's when I saw Frank. Word that I was in jail had spread from the Union of Nova Scotia Indians to all the reserves in Cape Breton. Frank found out about it somehow and came to be with me at the hearing. Because this was my first offense, I was fined twenty-five dollars. We paid the fine and rode home in the car. I remember Frank turned to me and said, "You must love me an awful lot to do that. It's the first time in your life that you've ever been arrested for doing something."

"Well," I said, "I was fighting for my family." For several months, we had been having a hard time. I told him the family just couldn't take it anymore. After that, he came home.

In a little while, I went to see the woman who had been involved with Frank and had a serious talk with her. I explained the situation, woman to woman, and that was more effective than the other way of doing things. I told her, "I have a little baby, and the other children are like steps — eight of them in a row."

She said to me, "I didn't know. I just thought that I was in love with the guy and I didn't consider the family." She told me not to worry anymore, and she became a friend instead.

Of course, everybody talked about what had happened, but I know how to live down things like that. I just ignored it and went on with my life. If people made fun of me or laughed, I would laugh along with them. I even laughed when they called me "Bonnie and Clyde" and all sorts of other crazy names. But the thing that drove me away from writing my column was being called "Here and There." When I heard that, I laughed, but I dropped the column. I didn't want to be given that nickname; I knew how nicknames stick.

Once in a while after this, I would write a story about someone I admired and send it to the paper. I learned to write in a loving and honourable way about people. I only wrote one bad story about a person and I got a lot of negative feedback on that. Most of the time I would write about someone who moved me.

For example, my friend Sarah Denny moved me. When her kids were small and my kids were small, we shared a lot of our problems — we were buddies. We were both women trying to keep our families together and worrying about cooking the next meal and experiencing hardship. It was like that everywhere I went — people always had the same problems and storytelling would come with the sharing of problems and medicine and baby-sitting and jokes. This is part of the friendly atmosphere I have always known amongst my people. So I would write about that.

Sarah Denny taught me many, many basic things about our culture. There are lots of things about our cultural traditions that I don't know, so I would ask women in the community for information. Sarah taught me about traditions such as giving a young Mi'kmaq woman a cone-shaped hat at the time of puberty.

> She is our culture
> Knowing all
> From birth to end
> The Christian song
>
> She is a Micmac
> Representing her call
> Pounding her drum in song
> And the art in telling is her draw
>
> She is our culture
> Knowing all
> My friend Sarah
> Relating our knowledge, we stand tall.

I wrote poetry on almost every subject I could think of, but, at that time, one thing I never wrote about was the battering I had experienced. I guess it was just fear of writing about things like that while my husband was alive. I didn't want to step on live toes; I still don't. The poems I wrote about people were always honourable.

■ ■ ■

By this time, Frank and I had settled into our life together again; we were involved with our family and our growing children. In high school, I worried about Phyllis. She was beautiful but so skinny that one boy teased her and called her "plywood." She was upset by that, but Frank told her to pay no attention and I told her to make the most of what she had. She followed that advice, and still does today.

> They have rock concerts in the community hall
> Dancing but not touching.
> Eyes focused on nothing special
> And a shy contact with the opposite sex.
> A friendly teasing with others their age,
> These are the young girls of Eskasoni.
>
> On Saturdays and Sundays
> They appear at church
> Along with the rest of their families
> With younger brothers and sisters
> Trailing admiration, conformity inspired.
> These are the young girls of Eskasoni
> Soon to be women.
>
> Most go for higher learning
> Not knowing what the future holds.
> But some are angry for their tomorrows
> In a mixed-up flow of ideas, not in bloom.
> These are the young girls of Eskasoni
> Soon to be women.

When Junior was in high school, I worried about him, too. Once, when he was sixteen, he announced that he was interested in another religion. The subject was delicate, so I just told him to remember that his father and I had taught him that the Creator existed, and that the main thing was to be good. He did not say anything to this, but later he was in a serious accident. Luckily, nobody was killed, and the next time we talked he said that now he knew who the Great Spirit was. My other son, Basil, I did not worry about so much. He had been slow when he was a child, but he was strong-willed. When he was about twelve years old, he saved a four-year-old child from drowning and received a Bronze Medal. The medal was a surprise to him; Frank and I made more noise about it than he did. He always tried his best at everything.

Phyllis was the first of my children to marry, when she was still in her teens; then, between 1970 and 1980, Step, Bernadette and Francis also married, and soon I had grandchildren in my home as well as children.

In 1973, when Ann was six and Caroline was ten, we took in some foster children — two little boys, six and eight years old. They were bad little boys. We had to lay down the law: no swearing or hitting in this house. I said to them, "I'll treat you the same way as I treat my own children — no better and no worse." The six year old — his name was Dana — was jealous of Ann, and Ann was jealous of the treatment I gave Dana. I told Ann that I had to hug Dana often because he had been in a lot of homes, like me when I was a child, and felt rejected. Nobody had wanted him until I got hold of him. So I would give him extra hugs. I knew that the only way you could teach people love is to give them love. Those boys still call me "Mom" today.

Around this time, my half brother William, who was now elderly, came to live with us for a while. After I had left Oxford when I was a child, William and Madeline had ended up in Maine, where they lived in very poor conditions. Madeline had died there, during a time when William was in jail for a minor offense. Finally, William came to live in Eskasoni, staying with us until a few short years before he died in 1981. I never told him why I had left Oxford; I think he assumed that the Indian Agent came and took me away. I just left it at that.

My husband loved my half brother very much, although he could never explain why. I guess William made an impression on Frank because he was a person who had lived for so long in awful conditions, but he was also a gentle person whose only mistake was alcoholism. When he lived with us, his love for my children was a sight to behold.

■ ■ ■

In December of 1973, Frank and I received word that my brother Matt Bernard had died of heart disease in Boston. Matt was only forty-six years old. My husband immediately left for Boston to accompany the body home to Cape Breton. There was to be a wake in Membertou, Matt's last home before he had moved to the United States.

I have always wished that I had known Matt better; I used to think he was bitter because he had not been close to the family from the time that he was a child. The night after Frank left, I lay awake thinking about my brother. One funny thing I remembered was that Matt had spoken English all the time, while my brother Roddy, who spent the same amount of time at Indian residential school, spoke Mi'kmaq. Whenever I had spoken in Mi'kmaq to Matt, he would answer in English; and whenever Roddy had tried to push Native culture on him, Matt would become angry.

I wondered why Matt had to die so young, after serving without mishap in the armed forces. After tossing and turning most of the night, I finally lay resting, although I was still awake. It was then that a tall figure walked into my bedroom, came to the left side of my bed and stooped over me as if to kiss me. I thought this figure was my husband, but at the same instant as I felt the kiss on my cheek I remembered that Frank was in Boston. I hollered, "Turn on the light," and the figure whispered, "Shhh." When I finally reached the light and turned it on, nobody was in the room. I ran to the other bedrooms and checked on my children and my elderly brother William; they were all asleep.

Matt must have come to give me his last goodbye, I decided. I was not afraid, because I had often heard my people say that if a person loves you in life, he will do so in death and will not frighten you.

When Frank returned the next night, I told him what had happened but he did not believe in such things. He went to bed and soon fell asleep, while I lay awake again, thinking of my brother. Soon, my husband began making noises in his sleep; I awakened him and asked him what was wrong. He had dreamt of a figure, Frank said, who had come to the left side of the bed and bent over him as if to speak. Just at that moment, I had woken him up.

I knew then that Matt had come to our house a second time, to prove his point to my skeptical husband.

In my bed one night I awoke to a sensation of touch
A man was peering down at me
As if with concern.
A beautiful jacket hung on his lean frame
The fringes swinging with every move
His stride the sureness of man.
The face I could not see, it was circled in fog
Then he turned, going through the wall.
I jumped out of bed in search of him
And seeing the secure door, knew he was supernatural.

■ ■ ■

It was in 1974 that I saw an item in the Cape Breton Post stating that there was a literary contest at the Writers' Federation in Halifax. By then, I had a lot of handwritten poetry stored away; my cousin Roy Gould, who was the editor of the *Micmac News*, had told me to always keep a carbon copy of anything I wrote. So I borrowed a typewriter from somebody and went to work on those poems.

My English was poor, and my words were frustrated, angry, crying, hoping for communication. I wrote about what I had experienced and what I now saw my children experience — the feeling of being immersed in an alien nation and culture.

I did not tell anybody that I had entered the contest. That way, if I didn't win, nobody would know. I always do things this way — even to this day, I never confide in anyone about a contest or anything unusual I may be pursuing. Then, if I fall face down, it will be my face in the dirt and nobody else's.

One day, a lady phoned me from the Nova Scotia Writers' Federation and told me that I was one of the winners of the poetry contest. I was dumbstruck. She said that there would be an awards ceremony and that I should be there to receive the prize. "May I come in Indian dress?" I asked.

"Of course!" the woman replied. She sounded happy; she was probably visualizing a beautiful Indian maiden in Native dress.

Once I was off the phone, I practically hollered at Frank, "I won! I won!"

His face was bland. "What did you win?" he said. Then I remembered that I had not told him about the contest. I explained what had happened and told him about the awards ceremony. His face lit up, thinking of the free booze and pretty women.

I loved that man, even knowing about his women. My heart felt as big as all outdoors. This was my own accomplishment, my personal triumph.

■ ■ ■

Though it was natural for me to create my leather dress
The beads and quill my ornamentation
You call it art.
It makes me feel wise with a sense of identity.

Though it was necessity, I used bone, stone and wood to
Carve my images.
You call it art.
It makes me feel wise and a seer of beauty.

Though I created the mask for mystical purposes
The amulets my ritual objects
You call it art.
It makes me feel wise as my spirit flows with love.

My sketches have revealed the loneliness of fading away
The message passing in the wind to all eternity.
You call it art.
My spirit shadow celebrates, "You have found me!"

Frank and I drove to the Holiday Inn in Halifax for the ceremony, me in my borrowed moccasins and Native dress of polyester with leather fringe. Oh, I felt so good; I even visualized riches beyond dreams.

When we arrived at the Holiday Inn, the place was packed with people. I noticed that the ladies all wore evening gowns or beautiful dresses; my polyester dress stuck out like a sore thumb.

Frank and I were led to a reserved table that held our name cards. We made polite conversation with the other people at the table as the evening began and the prizes were handed out in each category. Finally, the poetry category was announced. In my nervousness, I kept talking to the person next to me. Frank had to give me a poke when I was called. I remember walking to the front of the room, the announcement of my name music in my ears: "Rita Joe, from Eskasoni, Cape Breton." I accepted the award and floated back to my seat, the applause elevating my spirit.

The rest of the evening I spent with stars in my eyes, shaking hands, talking to everyone around me, enjoying the feeling of my triumph. I was a Native and I had won over other people — this is what I thought to myself. Who knows what may have swayed the judges? Maybe it was the fact that I was the lone Indian among all the intellectuals. But I really didn't care why I was chosen. I had won!

When Frank and I were preparing to come to Halifax for the ceremony, I had bought a book written by a woman I knew would be there. She was famous and her book was a bestseller. I had the idea in my mind that I would get her to autograph the book and ask her for tips on writing a bestseller. That evening, I looked around at all the people, but she was nowhere in sight. Soon Frank was nowhere to be found either, so I wandered into a dimly lit room that had been set aside for anyone who wanted to relax and have a drink. A band was playing in the corner of the room. I spotted some people I knew and asked if they had seen Frank. One of the women pursed her lips and indicated the dance floor: There were Frank and the famous writer glued together, dancing.

The green-eyed monster went to work within me straight away; then I remembered that the famous writer was the person I wanted to see. I told myself that first things come first — the monster could wait. When the dance ended, Frank and the writer came up to me. Frank introduced me: "My wife, Rita Joe."

"I have been wanting to meet you for the longest time," the writer announced. She came over to me and leaned on my shoulder. "I hope you did not mind me dancing with your husband?"

"*Mussy mon eta!*" I replied. This is an insult in Mi'kmaq. I could see my husband grinning like a cheshire cat. He was the only one who understood how rude I had been.

"What did you say?" asked the writer.

"Oh, I don't mind," I murmured, and we all sat down at our table and talked. "How did you do your research? Who did you ask?" I queried. I knew the content of her book inside out. There were many stories that I thought must have come from my own people.

"Indians," she confirmed.

"Aha!" I said. "You took it from the Indians." I mentioned certain paragraphs that I had read over and over again.

"You remember that?" she said, and we talked for a long time.

On our way home, Frank was curious. "What were you two discussing?" he asked. I told Frank that I was going to write a bestseller myself. He teased me and said, "I'll divorce you!" That announcement swelled my heart. I knew he loved me in his own way.

■ ■ ■

A little while later, the Writers' Federation of Nova Scotia offered to find a publisher for my work. This idea had not occurred to me, but the Writers' Federation looked around for a way to fund the project and a publisher was found.

An editor was hired, as well — an award-winning author who worked with me on structure, metaphor, synonyms and what-not. I did not understand much of what he said, but I did understand what Indians did or did not do. At one point, we had an argument about one of the poems. He kept saying, "That didn't happen!" He was trying to rile me up.

I answered this remark with an assertive outburst, "I lived it, damn it!" That was the spirit my helper was trying to bring out in me. I remember he told me, "Please explain more. You assume we know things that we don't know." Our exasperating afternoon ended with a cautionary remark from him that I live with to this day: "Rita, you are doing an awful lot of crying in your poetry. You cry too much."

I understood what this man was trying to say and from that time on I tried not to cry; I tried to be more assertive in my writing. I also tried to express myself more clearly. I no longer assumed that everyone knew about my culture. It took me a long time to understand this. I had been interviewed and researched so much — I don't know how many people have come onto the reserve and gone to every house asking questions. My people have been "researched" to death.

> The acted role of an Indian,
> A character assumed wrong.
> The continuous misinterpretations
> Of a life
> That is hurting.
>
> Echoes climb,
> Distorted
> Endlessly by repeated lies.
> An undertow of current time.

Will it ever die?
Loosen the bond.
Undo?
Will not this relating ease

So that we may rest,
Performance over
And unravel the mistake —
Stories told
Of Indians and white men.

I call *Poems of Rita Joe* my "cry and look at me" book. In it, I talked about honour and good intentions. If I said something negative, I followed it up with something positive. I was still afraid when I wrote that first book.

I am the Indian,
And the burden
Lies yet with me.

■ ■ ■

Poems of Rita Joe was published by Abanaki Press in 1978. I had no knowledge of book publishing and at first when the book was printed I didn't know where it was going or if it was making much money. I did know my husband was proud of the book and selling it at every opportunity. Finally, the Department of Education in my province made contact with me and asked if I wanted to speak in the schools.

The schools in Nova Scotia did not have much money, so when I gave a talk, I would receive a diary book or craft for payment. Then The Canada Council heard about me and contacted me to speak in different places. They would ask me half a year in advance. The schools, universities, women's groups and other organizations I spoke to kept me busy for the next several years.

I stand before the native children
Baring my soul about our culture.
I stand before them offering my last,
For that golden dream, and the ladder
We try to climb.

The maiden speech,
The dawn of that titled page
To open doors.

I bare my abilities to them
Stating the limits,
The all-important meaning
To tell our side,
The aspirations.

They listen:
A generation of cultural mend is born
I see it in their eyes
The healing art of smouldering interest.

At first, the scariest thing for me was speaking to a Mi'kmaq audience. I remember, one time, when I spoke to a University of New Brunswick class in Eskasoni. I shook like a leaf. "You guys scare me," I said, in Mi'kmaq. My friend Helen Sylliboy, who was a student in the class, handed me a glass of water. "Why do we scare you, Rita?" she asked. "We admire you." I thanked her for that from the bottom of my heart.

Sometimes Frank would be in the audience; he made me nervous, too. I always told my husband to hide behind somebody so that I would not catch his eye and laugh or keel over. He was my worst critic; it kept me on my toes. Later on, when he went back to school himself, he would say, "Rita, you have to know all about a subject to write about it." And my children would sometimes stand over me when I had a poem in front of me and say, "You spelled that word wrong, Mom."

I would say, "Never mind, never mind. It's a song!" I wasn't that worried about using correct English; I was worried about the song.

Listening to the women in my community helped me a lot in my writing and speaking, especially when I was just beginning. In fact, some of the well-known lines in the poems probably belong to them — expressed in Mi'kmaq and put into English when I wrote. Murdena Marshall, who teaches at the University College of Cape Breton, is someone I have relied upon from time to time. She uses the Mi'kmaq language to emphasize a point, especially at funerals or church or community functions. To me, the ultimate expression of any important issue is to voice it in Mi'kmaq — it moves me to hear the words. So, usually, when I hear something voiced in my first language, I listen very carefully then translate it into English.

Speaking to non-Native audiences was a different kind of experience than speaking to my own people. I remember once I was invited to Northern Ontario and I wanted to include an Indian song in my presentation. I asked my friend Sarah Denny, who was with the Micmac Institute of Cultural Studies, to teach me one of the songs she sings. The song she taught me has an "ego" sound in it. The night before leaving for my engagement, I called up Sarah and asked her how many "egos" there were in the song. "Never mind how many damn egos!" she said. "They won't know the difference where you are going." I laughed very hard at that because it is true that non-Indians know too little about Native expressions to spot the differences.

All my presentations were done with much care, no matter whether I spoke to six people or six thousand, to Natives or non-Natives. Eloquence is not always in my style, but if the spiritual part of things is evident in my words, the truth comes from the root of my being.

I remember one time when I was speaking at a police organization's function. There were lots of people gathered in the hotel where I was speaking. Earlier, a young Native man had gone on stage. He was in full regalia and he had a drum with him, and he was talking about Native culture. It was an interesting and honourable talk. But you could hear people murmuring to each other and laughing while he was on stage. It was a humiliating experience for the young man.

After he was finished, a young Native woman, Cathy Martin, went on stage and she played a drum and talked. Her words were very intelligent and interesting, but nobody was paying attention to her. I was listening to her, but I was also listening to the murmuring. Finally, the announcement came: "And now, the main speaker: Rita Joe."

I got up there and the first thing I did was slap the podium. Slam! You can imagine — it sounded like thunder. I slammed my hand down on the podium and I said, "You guys never listen! You never listen. You never listened for five hundred years and you're still not listening!"

Everything was still. My daughter Phyllis was there; it was her first experience in taking me somewhere to talk. She went out into the hallway. She knew I was angry and she didn't know what would happen. In the hallway she ran into a young police officer, and he was muttering, "Just like my mother." Phyllis laughed and told him, "That *is* my mother up there!"

After I had finished telling off the audience, I read from my book. Then I said, "You have to listen to us. If we want to tell you something, it must be heard. If it's not heard, you won't know what's going on with my people — or with any culture, I imagine. I guess that's why you're here in the first place. I guess you want to know about my people on the reserve — what they're up to and what their achievements are and what their honourable intentions are. And you should want to know. Because we're taking matters into our own hands."

> Justice seems to have many faces
> It does not want to play if my skin is not the right hue,
> Or correct the wrong we long for,
> Action hanging off-balance
> Justice is like an open field
> We observe, but are afraid to approach.
> We have been burned before
> Hence the broken stride
> And the lingering doubt
> We often hide

Justice may want to play
If we have an open smile
And offer the hand of communication
To make it worthwhile

Justice has to make me see
Hear, feel.
Then I will know the truth is like a toy
To be enjoyed or broken

■ ■ ■

On November 28, 1980, my brother Roddy disappeared.

After Roddy went into the army when I was still a little girl, I did not have very much contact with him. A long time after he enlisted we heard he was injured, and I saw him once when he was on crutches and wearing dark glasses. He later went blind in one eye and his hip injury hurt him for the rest of his life. He went to Boston when he was still a young man, and then I heard only small news about him.

In 1974, twenty years after I had last seen Roddy, I met him again while Frank and I were blueberry picking in Maine. I went over and hugged him; both of us had tears in our eyes. There was not a dry eye amongst anyone who looked on, either.

I saw him standing there
His dark hair tied back with a kerchief
He looked so Indian, so dear
I ran across the parking lot and hugged him
The people who saw us knew our story
Their eyes filled with tears
The long separation, while I looked after my family
He lived so far away
Until that day we met in Maine, U.S.A.

Roddy stayed blueberry picking with us for awhile, and he and Frank got along well. They were both boozers at that time. After awhile, my nerves became frazzled from seeing the drinking and working in the blueberry fields from dawn to dusk with my children. Finally, I packed our clothes and insisted we go home, and Frank did not argue with me.

After that, Roddy eventually came home, too. He stayed with us for awhile in Eskasoni, and he stayed with my brother Soln's family in Whycocomagh. By this time, Soln had grown children of his own, whom I loved very much, and we would visit each other's families. I have always wished that Roddy had married; I would have loved his children like I love Soln's.

Just a few months before he disappeared, Roddy had returned to Whycocomagh after being a patient in a nearby hospital. The last we heard of him, he had been acting out of the ordinary, but nobody took him seriously. To those around him, he was gentle and harmless. He had walked out into the deep water beside Whycocomagh, and when someone hollered to him, "What are you doing out there?" he had replied, "*Aklasiew* (white people) are chasing me." He had also taken an angelus bell from the church altar and stuffed it with tissue paper, explaining that each time the bell rang, someone died.

When Roddy could not be found on November 28, people thought that he may have taken a bus to Boston. In the next few days, people on all the reserves looked for him and we received calls from Boston and Maine Indians, but no one had seen him. I even consulted a seer; he told Frank and me, "The man you are looking for will not be found."

Soln was broken up when Roddy disappeared. The two brothers were very close to each other. Less than two months after Roddy disappeared, Soln died of heart disease, like Matt had. Roddy's body was not found until eight years later. He had died on Skye Mountain in Cape Breton in 1980. I arranged his funeral and now he lies in Eskasoni.

I loved my two brothers very much; they were always good to me. I remember the last time they came to visit me in Eskasoni. Soln was following Roddy down the stairs into my basement kitchen. "Roddy, you are slow like a *mikjij*!" I heard him say, teasing.

"What is a *mikjij*?" I asked.

"A turtle," I was told.

My kitchen is now upstairs, but every time I'm in the basement of my house I visualize my two brothers walking in, with Roddy in the lead and Soln complaining, "You are slow like a *mikjij*." And then I smile, because the love is still there.

> On November 28, 1980, my brother Roddy disappeared.
> No one knew where he went, what he thought
> What pain he felt, or if he was scared.
>
> All through the years we wondered
> Through discussions among kin.
> Was he alive?
> Is he dead?
> Or just a breath away.
>
> On August 25, 1988, the realization became fact.
> He was found, where he lay down so long ago.
> Deaf to the past, no wish for the future
> Or extremely sad.
>
> No one knows.
> But through visions in our dreams he communicated,
> Apologetic for leaving, expressing love to all.
> He lived, he died.
> Whatever he couldn't say on earth
> Now he sends pictures in our mind's eye.

■ ■ ■

When *Poems of Rita Joe* first came out, the media called it literature and praised it. Frank looked up some of the words the reviewers used. "It says here you're a genius," he told me.

"I'm no genius," I said. "I'm just stating the facts of life." That shook him.

My immediate reaction to the praise was to try to better my education. Over the following two years, I got my Grade Twelve high school diploma and I took a course in business education. I learned to type using all my fingers. In 1980, I even began to mention a college degree. "I think I'll go to college if they're calling me a literary genius. I've got to catch up," I joked to Frank.

Around that time, my husband walked into the house one day and expressed a desire for higher learning himself. "By all means, go ahead!" I said, feeling excited for him. Frank was a proud man, and I built him up: He had the best legs, the best hair, the best everything. I learned this early in life: When you praise somebody, goodness is returned to you. So when he told me he was going to college, I supported him. I also said to myself, "Oh my *Niskam* (God), you have heard my prayer for Frank. If the real Frank is ready to be tested, the day will be his."

At the same time, our daughter Step's marriage to a Whycocomagh police officer was breaking up. She also expressed her desire to better herself, but she had a four-month-old baby to consider, as well as two older children. I no longer had small children at home — just teenagers, Ann and Caroline. I put my own dream on the shelf for awhile and looked after the three little ones.

Three years later, Step received her degree from Teachers College; in four years, my husband finished his degree at the University of New Brunswick. I was so proud of both of them. Frank was not satisfied with his Bachelor of Education degree, though; there was still more that he wanted to do. He went to work for the Micmac Family and Children's Services, which was just starting up at that time, and began a sociology degree. He kept encouraging Step to upgrade her education as well — the two of them had heavy discussions about everything. I would listen to them, my heart swelling with pride.

At last, the job and the higher learning brought Frank satisfaction of a need that had been bursting out of him all those years. The four years that he worked for the Micmac Family and Children's Services and went to school were hard on him, but he said, "Even if I die after I finish the sociology degree, I'll be happy. A legacy will be left for our children and their children."

There are roles of conduct that stir the mind
And people sleeping a long time.
Why do they awaken?
They see a way:
Their thoughts breathe
Their words dance on the page
Their power to ease the heart
In lifting the soul to help
Across this country, this age.

There are forces in action
Calming the land.
Restoring the pieces of a mother's heart
Comforting the lonely child's want
Replacing the need of the caressing hand
And worth to a father image.
He is needed, he wept dry tears
Restoring the image, to the rising generation.

My life changed during these years, too. When Frank went to
school and got his Bachelor of Education and then his Sociology
degree, he had a great realization about our hardship together. He cut
out drinking altogether. His expressions of affection were never-ending, to make up for being mean in the earlier part of our marriage. He
was so good to me, forever telling me of his sorrow for his actions. In
the last years of our life together, there was so much love given and
expressed between us; that man could not do enough for me.

One conversation from that time still sticks out in my mind.
It occurred when Frank was earning his second degree. One day,
we drove into town in the truck and we were parked somewhere,
just talking, like husband and wife. He said to me, "I don't know
what I'm doing getting all these degrees. I don't know if I'm
crazy, or what. Why am I doing it?" The way I look back on it
today, he was fishing — fishing for compliments.

So I looked at him and I said, "You're not crazy. That's the
most intelligent thing you have ever done in all your life. It has
made you a better man. You have always been a good man, but
it has made you even better."

And Frank looked at me with a strange expression. I'll never forget that expression. He looked at me and said, "You know why I did it?"

I don't know what I was expecting to hear, but it was not what he said. He said, "I wanted to be better than you."

That shocked me. Why was this man trying to be better than me? I told him right then and there, "Don't ever, ever think that again as long as you live. You are a good man on your own. And you cannot be better than any other individual."

I was shocked, because I truly did not want to hear Frank say such things. I wanted him to know that he was on the same level as me. I wanted that so badly because it is a part of traditional Native belief. I remember I told him, "You know, nobody's in a higher position than the other person. Always, always, we're on the same level. I haven't got your education and you haven't got my expertise in poetry, but we look at each other on the same level. So don't ever let me hear you say that again."

After this, we had an unspoken agreement not to say anything about the hard times in our past. Sometimes, if I would mention something, he would say, *"Muk atukoiew* (Don't speak of legends)." And if he said anything about my earlier life, I would say the same: Don't speak of legends. One time, I told him that if we speak of past things, our sins weigh a ton.

My heart was full for this man I had been with for thirty-five years. Our children had felt fear, love and respect for their father, and finally they felt a great admiration. The admiration is what they carry in their hearts now.

It is because of this admiration that my daughters could not accept the abuse that occurred in their own marriages. They knew what had happened with me, and they still loved their father, but they would not accept the abuse for themselves or their children. All my daughters who experienced abuse from their husbands ended the marriages afterwards. Only Frances did not experience this — she married Tom Sylliboy, who is a good man. I love him like a son.

I wrote one poem about Frank that told some of the negative and some of the positive things about our life. I read it out to him, and he felt good about it. "You're telling the truth," he said. "You're telling what hardship we have." We cleared up our problems, our canoe floated along — this is what I said in the poem. I showed it to some of our children and read it out to them and they hugged me, because it's a good story, a good poem. It's about a man I loved, who also loved me, but who carried around his own little bundles.

> I first met him, he came knocking on my door
> Looking for his cousins in Boston in 1953.
> In time we married, a family we had.
> I remember he worked in construction
> Surgery attendant in a Boston hospital
> An orderly in Halifax
> A nursing attendant to Sydney we came.
> From there he became a labourer
> To construction again
> A field-worker for drugs and alcohol
> A band councillor, an iron-worker
> Even auctioneering after funerals
> Working for others to ease their pain.
> Then one day declaring the return to school
> To earn a degree, Bachelor of Education.
> To me, admiration became my day.
> Though there were ups and downs
> Our boat sailed along
> To each of us, our children and grandchildren,
> Hard work for canoe and paddle.
> Then if we make uneven waters, the going easy,
> It is because of the man who came, giving his name
> That precious knock on the door.
> What we are today we earned
> To better our tomorrows
> Using the gift of love and his fair name.

■ ■ ■

After my first book, I became braver in my writing. I grew less afraid to step on toes. But it took me a long time to write the second book. There were ten years between *Poems of Rita Joe* and *Song of Eskasoni*. When *Song* was published by Ragweed Press in 1988, another writer, Silver Donald Cameron, asked me, "What took you so damn long?"

"Oh," I said, "I can't keep up with you — a book every year!" It was true that I was very busy after the first book, travelling to different places and speaking, but I was insecure, too. A positive thing about going to all the speaking engagements is that I met other writers. Writers are good people and their hardships are many. Sometimes we would compare pitfalls and laugh about them. Silver Donald Cameron's support for the shy woman expressing her culture was very much appreciated. Many times I would go to a conference or speaking engagement and I would be the only Native person there. I would try to blend in, examine the topics to be discussed so as to be ready to give my input. But I was often lonely and thinking to myself, "Will they accept my opinion?" It would become like a game to me, to put forward my opinion, although I am not an aggressive person. I wanted to feel attachment to the group, to explain my perspective. Many times there would be interest, and sometimes I would feel shut out. If I was shut out, I always knew why; it was because the people did not know much about my culture, and whose fault was that? Still, I would try to tell as many stories as possible, try to fill the gap. Only once, at an economic conference in Sydney, did I feel so frustrated that I said to my granddaughter, who was with me, "Let's get out of here!" She took me to bingo; at least people talk to you there.

In the ten years between books, my research into my culture grew stronger. *Song of Eskasoni* is more assertive; the analysis of my culture takes on a different form. I vented my anger about what the world chooses to deny of my peoples' expression and history. I talked about what I knew to be true. In this second book, I was at war — but it was a gentle war. Showing anger is not ever to my liking. I try to sway people to see my point, to see my views concerning the Indian. I call my words a chisel, carving an image. Our image has been knocked down for too long by the old histories and old chronicles. The beauty in our expression and culture is there if one looks for it. The Métis poet Pauline Johnson found it long ago. I knew that if I searched long enough, I would find it too. That's what my second book was about; and that's why some people call me the warrior poet.

When I wrote my second book, and into my third, I analyzed my history and my talk. I wasn't afraid any longer; I didn't give a damn what the historians said about us. One of the things that I talked about in my second book was the Native writing that I had heard about and seen ever since I was a little girl. I knew Native writing was in existence — stone writings, I call them. My people had left a message in petroglyphs, but nobody who came after us could read it, so they chose to deny its existence. I also tried to study between the lines in the history books, and that searching has brought me the most satisfying conclusions. For instance, I was looking through an historical text about people called the "cross-bearers." A sentence mentioning the "Souri-quois" leaped out at me, and I knew from what I read that it referred to us, the Mi'kmaq. I had a tremendous feeling of discovery. "That's us!" I hollered in my kitchen. I did a jig to no one but my own spirit.

Soon after this, I read a book called *Extinction*, about the Beothucks in *Taqmku'k* (Newfoundland). I started to read it in my kitchen, and I read it and reread it, paragraph by paragraph. I looked at the way it was written and what it said. As I always do when I'm reading about Native people, I would say to myself, "This is not what happened. But this is what may have happened." I analyze my history that way. I was halfway through this book when I had to attend a meeting in Moncton. So I took the book along. When I got there, I finished reading it. I remember it was in the middle of the afternoon and I was in my room at the hotel, and I wanted to finish the book because I had to go to the meeting in the evening. I came to the end, where Demasduit's husband is killed because he lifts up a branch in a gesture of peace.

That moved me so much; it made me angry, sorrowful, emotional. My emotions took over, and I threw the book to the other side of the room and jumped up and looked out the window. I looked up at the sky and said, "They may have killed you, but they didn't kill your spirit." I spoke those words directly to Demasduit's spirit.

In March 1819, the Beothucks were surprised and killed.
Demasduit survived.
She had just given birth to a babe
All mothers on earth consider a prize.
A man, her captor, the all-powerful white
Committed a crime
Nobody paid.
Chief Nonosbawsut, her husband, tried with his life
But nobody paid.
I implore for Demasduit,
Mary March they named her,
I implore, know her,
But not her killer.
Know Demasduit
The last of the Beothucks of *Taqmku'k*.

One day, after my son Junior read about the Beothucks, he said to me, "Mom, the Beothucks did not all die. Remember these words from the book: *Pi'tow'ke'waq na nin* (We are from upriver). Those words are a clue." We knew from analysis of that phrase that the "Beothuck" might be Mi'kmaq; in fact, I would lay my life on the line that they were Mi'kmaq. I talked to people in my community about this, and my friend Murdena Marshall told me that her mother-in-law remembered an old woman in Conne River, Newfoundland, who would say, "*Pi'tow'ke'waq na nin* (I am from upriver)," when she was asked who she was. Also, an elderly man in Eskasoni told me that the word *Pi'tow'ke* means "upriver." The way I reason it, when my people encountered non-Natives they would repeat, "*Pi'tow'ke'waq na nin* (We are from upriver)." From those words came the similar-sounding word, "Beothucks."

I also knew from Frank's family that Natives in this area travelled back and forth by canoe between Cape Breton and Newfoundland. When Frank first went to university, he and I had both done some backtracking and researched our ancestors from the stories we had heard. My husband talked about his father, who would transport furs from Port aux Basques in Newfoundland to Louisbourg in Cape Breton. It was an established route. My mother-in-law would talk about it too. In the summer, it was easy to travel east, and in the winter people would sometimes walk long distances across the ice.

While Frank researched his heritage in Newfoundland, I found more information about the Goulds in Cape Breton. Of course, Frank thought my ancestry was funny. "The famous culture crazy found out she's not all there!" is how he put it.

"Your Newfoundland history is not so solid either," I shot back. We laughed about it all, but sometimes I wonder about the explanations that sweep through the ages.

Once, I was told that I would have the historians up in arms over the Beothucks, but I tell the historians: This is my history; this is one of the subjects I have heard my people talk about.

"I'm a Beothuck," my son announced.
"They didn't all die like history says."

My husband Frank Joe, his roots were from *Taqmku'k*
His father Stephen Joe came across looking for a wife
And he married a Micmac from *Po'tlo'tek*
Producing two girls and two boys,
One of them my husband.

Today my children dream of their ancestry
Being Beothuck, the grain flowing in them
I let them dream, even encouraging a possibility
Because I wonder, perhaps they were not all erased
And that speck of sand flows in my children.

I celebrate when I find out honourable things about my culture. I've spent a lot of time on it. One of the things I keep saying is that we are the ones who know about ourselves.

The words the non-Natives heard the Natives use have been misinterpreted throughout recorded history. If you are a Native speaking your language to non-Natives, you repeat yourself over and over, trying to be understood. This is how many of the places in our country got their names. To a Native person going through the countryside, Indian place names are a record of our explanations to non-Natives, our jokes and humour. We reason out what the Native person must have been saying, and what the non-Native person must have heard and misunderstood.

I talked to others who knew about my people, too. I remember, early in my writing career, I read a book of legends written by Ruth Holmes Whitehead. I did a review of the book. As I read what she had to say, I thought to myself, "This woman knows more about us than we know ourselves, because she is a museum curator and an anthropologist." But, after the review, I met her and she has been a good friend for many, many years. We communicate with each other. In my review of her work, I wrote: "*E'e*, the stories are good. A smile comes to my heart and I say to Ruth Holmes Whitehead: My world is like your world, the creative processes hanging in time, to be picked up by someone and put into effect to show that you have found me." Now, when I need to know something, I call Ruth; and when she wants to know something, she calls me.

> Somewhere there I have a friend
> The archives are her trade,
> A chronicler bringing nobility
> Together we relate the wonders of my nation,
> Our song a landing place.

■ ■ ■

In 1987, several years after Soln had died and Roddy had disappeared, my sister Annabel died of heart failure. I was very sad to lose her along with my brothers. We had shared a lot of growing-up stories, and she and John Ginter did a good job of raising Eddy, the son I had given them before moving to Boston long ago. Eddy had a secure family life, and this led him to have high standards. He become a family man himself and obtained his

Industrial Electrical Certificate. Annabel's only child of her own, Clarence, grew up to be a nice fellow, with a college degree under his belt.

Annabel and John had an intense togetherness, sometimes rocky but full of love. Although John used to tease me about my spiritual beliefs when I was younger, in later years he had more sympathy. Then he died, and Annabel's world fell apart. Whenever I saw her, I knew she was drinking. I was worried about her, so when Frank had to go to a conference in Truro, I asked him to drive the extra distance and visit Annabel in Halifax. I did not know it at the time, but this was just before her death. Frank said Annabel talked a long time, unloading her problems. Shortly after he left, she died on the street in Halifax, on her way to see the doctor.

> I held her in my arms
> Her flood of tears soaking my shoulder.
> I listened to her lament of reasons
> The continuous row of excuses for her drinking.
>
> My heart ached for the love I felt for her
> Trying to solve the problem I considered ours.
> She was my sister, I loved her very much.
> But I could not convince her
> That the many illnesses troubling her
> Were the result of alcohol.
> "No," she would say,
> "I haven't had a drink in a month."
> I held her close and let her cry
> Accepting the fact of what will happen and why.
>
> I went home to my family and promised myself
> I would tell them I love them every day.
> They are beautiful, ambitious, intelligent
> All the things to lighten my heart.
> The words of trust, faith, I love you:
> To her there were none, only the bottle
> And finally the end.

Today, all I have is a memory
A sadness I recall.
Someone who was a part of my life is no more
Because of the cursed alcohol.

Today, I remember our closeness when we were young, how Annabel was my older sister, always looking out for the younger one. She used to tell me I was blessed with all my babies, because she only had the one little boy of her own. I think of her and realize that I had a wonderful sister who tried as hard as she could to be a mother to me.

■ ■ ■

Between 1980 and 1989, as Frank and I grew older, the spiritual part of our togetherness became stronger. We would go together to many of my speaking engagements; I would call them "our little honeymoons."

I remember his words to me on the last little honeymoon we took in Maine, in August 1989. "Are you happy?" he asked.

"I'm happy where you are," I told him.

"I'm happy where you are, too," he said.

It was a Sunday, so we went to a little church at Peter Dana Point in Maine. During the church service, I usually bow my head when the priest lifts the wafer. That morning, I looked at my husband's bowed head instead. Now, when I close my eyes, I see the bowed head.

"We're going to bingo!" my husband announced after the service. There was a bingo hall nearby, in Princeton. We had lunch there and settled into playing the game. A friend we knew from Shubenacadie sat near us and I remember Frank asked her if she knew where the Smithsonian Institute was. "What in the world do you want with that place?" I asked.

"That's the place where I'm taking you next," he said. I replied that the trip we had taken to Niagara Falls earlier was enough for me.

That evening, we got a room near Calais, Maine. The manager of the place had a French name. Frank said to him, "You know that they took the land from us, don't you?" The man understood Frank's expression of solidarity. "They did at that," he said and the two became fast friends. "You two are good people," he told us.

When we were settling in for the night, Frank was restless. "I'm going to get some lunch," he said.

"Lock the door behind you," I told him, "because I'm taking a shower and going to sleep." During the night, I awoke a few times and saw Frank sitting up. "Go to sleep," he would say. Each time, I rolled over and went back to sleep.

In the morning, I tried to get up without waking Frank, but he opened his eyes. "What time did you finally get to sleep?" I asked. "After the sixth Tum," he replied. He got up and asked me to make tea while he showered.

I made the tea and put raisin bran in a bowl for him. I could hear him in the shower; I remember he hollered when the hot water ran out. "How do I look?" he asked afterwards, standing before me in a very white shirt and tan-coloured pants.

"*Me'tasimon* (You smell romantic)."

"Oh, you're just saying that," he said and we both laughed, happy in our togetherness. He lifted a small bag. "I'll put the stuff in the car while you clean up."

In a moment, I heard the car door slam. Frank came inside, holding his chest. "*Ke'snukay*, Rita (I'm sick, Rita)."

"Sit down. I'll put the stuff in the car."

Frank sat on the edge of the bed and his eyes told me of the pain he felt. Then the look in them told me of the love he had for me and his sadness in leaving me. He fell back on the bed.

I ran outside. The cleaning lady for the rooms was there. "Call an ambulance," I yelled at her. I ran back in to Frank. As I stood over him, waiting for his convulsion to pass, I saw him sigh and relax. I felt a whiff of cold air, as if it was passing through me. Without thinking, I even raised my eyes to the ceiling, expecting to see Frank's passing. Then, "*Kogo'ey wejinkalin'* (Why did you leave me)?" I hollered at the still form.

I ran outside again, yelling to no one in particular, my sorrow and anger mingled together.

At the hospital, the doctors met me. I could see the "no" in their eyes. "I want to call home," I told a nurse. She dialed the Canadian exchange and our daughter Caroline answered the ring. "Your father is ill," I said. I heard her call out to her younger sister Ann, "Dad is sick." Then the nurse tapped me on the shoulder, indicating that a doctor wanted to tell me something and I should hang up.

"You do not know what this man has done!" I repeated, over and over. I meant that these strangers did not know how much Frank Joe had accomplished.

In a while, a social worker came and we talked for a long time. The Chief of Eskasoni, Allison Bernard, was called. He and some other people from Eskasoni were working in Maine, in a nearby blueberry field. I told him to make sure that my daughter, Frances, who was also working at the blueberry camp, was notified of the death before someone blurted it out accidentally. Allison later told me that he pitied Frances, standing there with a beautiful smile on her face, not knowing that her father was dead.

Allison came to pick me up and take me to Frances. I remember he was eating an apple. I knocked it out of his hand, exclaiming, "You men are always eating!" Poor man, he left that apple on the ground.

When we arrived at the blueberry camp, Frances came running over to me. Our tears soaked each other's shoulders. Frances' husband, Tom, took command and found a driver to take my car back to Canada. Tom's mother passed the word around about Frank. Soon, a bundle of cash was handed to me. "Gas money," Tom's mother said.

My grandson, Oliver Jr., drove me back to Eskasoni, while my son-in-law followed in a truck with Frances and their three children. I sat there, reliving my pain, looking at Frank's identification card. "He's a good man, who knows many trades, one of them being social worker for the Children's Services," I told my *Niskam* (God).

• • •

The day of Frank's burial and funeral auction made me realize
again the immense appreciation I feel for my people. The funeral
auction is a customary practice where the deceased's personal
belongings and donations from the people are gathered together
and auctioned. Sometimes, people will give the last of their
money to the auction. When it is over, the funeral bills are paid
and anything that is left goes to the family. Even today, I look
around at my people at *salite'* (the funeral auction), and see how
good they are, practicing the simple act of helping another
individual in need. It reminds me of my tradition, of how, a long
time ago, we would help each other by feeding the crowd, giving
comfort, doing any small deed that we knew in our hearts would
help survivors.

A month after Frank died, I received an answer to my prayer
to *Niskam* (God). One of my daughters wrote to me: "I dreamt
about Dad. He was holding a baby and his hair was the colour of
snow." The colour white is a symbol of peace in my culture. I
knew Frank was at peace.

> On the morning of August 14, 1989
> My husband Frank passed away in Calais, Maine.
> The thirty-five years we spent together
> Is a love story in itself, always there.
> I respected the man and lost him
> *Ki'su'lk weswalata.*

• • •

The day after Frank's funeral, I asked one of my sons to take me
to Tatamagouche, where I had agreed to speak. My engagement
there was supposed to be with Frank; now, I started my world
without him.

I also thought to myself, "I'm going to write the truth from
now on." I still do not like to step on live toes and I'm still working
on a positive outlook. But I said to my children, "If I speak about

myself, I'm going to tell the truth. Maybe it will hurt you sometimes, because I'm going to talk about the wrong I have done and things that have hurt me, but I will talk about it openly from now on."

"There's nothing about your life that we have not experienced ourselves, Mom," one of my daughters told me. "All of us who are women — we all experience negative things sometimes."

It was only then that I wrote a poem about being a battered woman; it was later included in my third book. I also started writing about my life. One of my daughters was looking at what I had put down, and she laughed and said, "By God, there's a lot of things we don't know about you, Mom."

Another daughter was reading something over and said, "Mom! You're swearing in here!" My children follow their father in not cursing or swearing. Frank used to drink, but he didn't swear. I didn't swear often, but I tried to tell the truth about when I did. My children laughed most of all when I wrote about my jealousy over Frank at the literary awards.

I wrote these things down because I did not want to erase what had happened in my life or what I saw happen in other peoples' lives. I think my children were surprised at first to see things in print, even if they had known about them all along.

■ ■ ■

On December 23, 1989, I was notified that I was to be a recipient of the Order of Canada. Quietly, I thanked the lady who phoned me. I remember she kept asking me if I was excited. "It is like a Christmas gift from the country," I replied, "but I would be more excited if my husband could be with me."

When I got off the phone, I sat down on a chair and looked at my family members. "I wish your father were here to hear the news," I told them.

"He knows," they all chorused. My children were proud of my accomplishment; they had had a part in it, too. Many a time I did not wash or cook or do the things I was supposed to do because I'd be at the typewriter, writing my stories. Even my Mother's Day gifts were typing paper, carbon paper or a thesaurus. My children knew the determination and will I had put into my work, and honouring that will made their contribution even more positive.

I felt good inside. To me, the acknowledgement from my country meant that they were returning a gift to me. It was a salute to the Aboriginal people of the land. I gave thanks to my Creator; I could not have produced my gift without the spiritual belief I hold in my heart.

One day just before I was supposed to go to Ottawa to receive the award, I went into Sydney to look for a nice hat. A woman in one of the stores said to me, "Are you the lady I've been hearing about all day on the radio?"

"I am, yes," I said, offering my hand. She did not take it.

"And where did you go to university?" she asked.

My gaze held her steely eyes as I explained that I had not gone to any college, but that now I spoke at many of them. My bubble of happiness about the award almost burst — but I would not let it. The dreary war never ends, I thought. Perhaps my award rubbed her the wrong way; maybe she expected a more educated person to be compensated by our country. Maybe someday I will be brave and offer my hand again.

> I walk into a store in town
> My pockets bursting with money
> My needs are like any other
> For goods I want to buy in a hurry
> The clerk in the store sees my face, the rugged clothes
> My feet in mukluks, the headband on my brow
>
> She has immediate ideas of the poor Indian,
> The stereotype in progress
> She does not know I sense ill will
> So gently I turn around and walk out,
> Looking for another store

One where the clerk is all smiles, even if it hurts.
I have bought out the store,
My pockets empty.
Prejudice is something we can do without
Accept me just as I am,
My money, and my identity.

Finally, it was time to travel to Ottawa to receive the award. My daughter Caroline offered to go with me and we packed the few basic things we would need. I looked at the two Native garments I owned: Which should I wear? In the end I decided to take them both so that Caroline could wear one, too.

On the plane to Ottawa I was surprised to be put into the First Class section; then, when the plane was airborne, the pilot's voice came over the intercom: "We have two special ladies on board on their way to Ottawa. One of them is Rita Joe, who is receiving the Order of Canada!" There was applause, and the stewardess came forward to lead us into the cockpit to shake hands with the pilot and co-pilot. I was more fascinated to see the front of the plane than anything else, but the card I received from the pilot I still treasure to this day.

Finally, we arrived in Ottawa and were escorted to an elegant hotel. The next morning, both Caroline and I were excited. Caroline had a smile on her face that I recognized; it meant that she was up to something. "*Menaqa tlitute'n* (Act correctly)," I advised her again and again. I loved her so dearly from the day she was born, with her large dark eyes and black hair, and I knew that her straight-forward attitude could sometimes get her into trouble. The apprehension I felt was for nothing. The only thing she did was call me "Mother Ambassador," drawing grins from her listeners.

An aide at the Governor General's residence advised us on proper bearing when meeting the Prime Minister and the Governor General. The correct bearing did not matter to me. "These people are just like me," I thought. "Their rank is all that separates us." This belief did not let me down. Caroline and I met a lot of good people that day, and I felt honoured by everyone.

At the ceremony, I realized that I was no longer afraid to speak. I had met the leaders and educators, and I had no fear of them. I thought to myself, "I am the ambassador for my people here; if I do not have fear, my people will have no fear."

I had crossed a bridge: I did not feel insecurity anymore. Representing my people gave me a natural high; just reading from a poem or singing an Indian song with the drum made me happy. So many people had helped me in that. The applause I was given in 1974 when I won a prize for my poetry helped me start across. But you have to be brave yourself to make it to the other side.

In one of my poems, I thank my country for the honour they have given me; but I believe in my heart that it has the most meaning for the coming generation.

> The bus arrives at Rideau Hall
> The home of the Governor General of Canada.
> The place seemed the most inaccessible of all
> But here I am on April 18, 1990
> To receive an award.
> The recipients are led to their seats
> An aide gives direction about protocol
> All around we are polite with one another
> Everybody with their own thoughts.
> From the last row the names in sequence are called;
> Finally the man next to me is receiving.
> I start to shiver, my hands sweat.
> I know I'm going to stumble, thinking to myself
> *"Niskam apoqnmui'."*
>
> "Frank, are you there? I'm happy! Are you?"
> These are the things we used to say to each other
> It seems such a short time ago.
> "Rita Joe": I hear the name.
> I do not remember rising, a floating sensation
> Until I stand before the Governor General of Canada.
> He pins the medal, "The Order of Canada."
> I look into his eyes; they are kind.

"Thank you," I murmur.
I sign the register
And staring into peoples' eyes, searching for wonder
They shine, receiving my answer.
To me, the medal is for my people, the coming generation.
The greeting of the hand over the heart has earned a
    merit.
Thank you, my country, for accepting my salutation.

MY SONG (THE SPIRIT PATH)
(1990 —)

NTAPEKIAϘN

In the early morning hour
Many of us do a sweat in the sweatlodge
My *Kisulkw* is on my mind while doing the sweat.
Many hours later we finish, I am tired.
Somebody tells me to lay down and sleep under a tree.
I lay down with no care in the world, soon asleep.
One hour later I awaken and look at the sky.
I see a man dancing with a mandela in his hand
And an honour stick in the other.
He is in full regalia
Dancing, dancing.
I lift my arms to the sky, giving thanks
I have had a vision
I have seen something very few people see
I have see the Dancing Eagle
My *Kisulkw* in the sky.

My daughter Phyllis and I are going to Shubenacadie. As we drive past the hill where the residential school used to be, I point and Phyllis, who is driving the car, comments, "Where we both went." We look away quickly and head to the edge of town, where an old road leads to the Mi'kmaq reserve. Upon our arrival, we can hear the drums in the multi-purpose building. My heart starts to thump wildly, the strains of the song setting my senses to fast-forward, my longings cemented at last. I walk into the building with caution, though; the Parkinson's Disease which now troubles me is apparent in my steps and I have to be careful or I will stumble.

Inside, the drumbeat is familiar and my feet itch to get out onto the floor. I look around, hoping to see a face I know and say hello. I see a group of people who are standing around, and then I see a man dance past me, heading for the dance floor. He is not familiar, but I feel something as he passes by. The feeling is spiritual; it nudges my senses. "Who is the man dancing?" I ask someone, but they don't know. I make a mental note to meet the man later on. Now, the drumbeat is like a magnet for me, so I head for the floor, closing my eyes as I pray for the people who dance with me. I am dancing the *Kisikuisk* dance (the Old Woman dance) — the slow shuffle with the feet flat on the floor. The visual images in my head bring me a good feeling — the image of my people dancing as they always have. It is our form of prayer to *Kisulkw* (the Creator), the great spirit known to us since the dawn of time.

Later, the man I did not recognize is introduced to me. I shake his hand, wondering who he is; I can feel the strength of his spirit. It is explained to me that he is a pipe-carrier, a very good man. I don't doubt it one bit; I am satisfied. I wonder to myself what would happen if I placed a bit of tobacco in front of him and asked a question — any question. Perhaps the answer would surprise me at first, but eventually I would discover its meaning. My tobacco is ready for when we meet again.

■ ■ ■

Today, it seems like I walk down the middle lane of many roads. I walk the lane stemming from my roots: on the one hand, the crying part of me, begging you to understand how good my people are; on the other, the spiritual part of me remaining uppermost in my mind, reminding me of my path. More than anything else, I have been afraid to write about the spiritual part of things; Native spirituality is not easily understood.

Let me tell you about my first sweatlodge. We were all female, thirteen of us — one child and twelve grown women — and I was the eldest. A women's sweatlodge is more powerful than the men's. Some of us had never done the sweatlodge before and we were fascinated to find out what would happen. There is nobody to teach us what was traditionally done. We have had to discover it for ourselves, by observing and listening to others, and by doing things ourselves.

I was told to go in first, because I was the eldest; the others would follow according to their age. So I crawled into the enclosed area of the sweatlodge on my hands and knees and asked, out loud, for my ancestors to help me. The enclosed area is not even as high as I am; I couldn't stand up in it. But it is big and round and there is a pit in the middle for the heated rocks. When we were all inside, the door was closed and we started the first of four formations. Each formation lasts twenty minutes, and after each one another hot rock is put into the lodge and we are given a little water to drink.

I happened to be sitting alongside Donna Augustine, from Big Cove, New Brunswick, who was leading the sweatlodge. She was the first to speak, asking for spiritual help. The stones in the pit were very, very hot and, oh, I was sweating. It was like a very hot sauna. I was doing my own thing in my mind: I was talking, not aloud but to myself, in my own way — a spiritual way. My eyes were closed and I could hear the others speaking, one by one, and I kept hearing something else as well. I didn't understand this other sound. It seemed to me like eagles' wings flapping; it was powerful. In my own explorations, it was something that I was doing to myself; but, at the same time, I knew that what I was hearing was not the same sound as the one I was making. I could not explain this to myself, and I realized something spiritual was happening.

Finally, the door opened and we were given a bit of water. In a few minutes, another rock was placed in the pit. When the door opened I couldn't wear my glasses because they fogged over. You're not allowed to wear a watch or anything with metal — not even your bra — because the metal will burn your skin. So I had a baggy old dress on, and the sweat was just pouring off me. One of my daughters was sitting alongside me and another daughter was sitting at the door. They kept asking me, "Mom, do you want to leave now?"

"No, no," I said. I wanted all four formations. "Close the door." So we began the second formation — another twenty or twenty-five minutes. Again, I could hear the sound, and something unusual began to happen. Without my thinking about it or doing anything to make it happen, my hand began to lift up and then drop, lift and drop. This happened four times, before I finally said, "Leave me alone! You are hurting me." I was talking to the spirits that were doing this to me. Of course, I was perfectly safe; they were just telling me that they were there. After that, I had a feeling of great peace and goodness. I would ask a question in my head, and immediately an answer would come to me.

When I finally came out of the sweatlodge, I was still sweating; everyone was soaking wet from the sweat. I was looking around for my terrycloth robe to put over my baggy dress because I didn't want to get a chill. So I asked one of my daughters, "Do you know where my robe is?" and she looked at me and said, "Mom, you're not wet!"

I noticed for the first time that I was no longer soaked. I still don't know what happened, because when I was inside the sweatlodge, I could feel the sweat trickling down my back. I looked around and saw that there was one other woman who was dry, too. She didn't notice at all; she was too busy holding on to the way you feel when you come out.

When you come out you feel pure. Everybody was hugging me, but all the while I had this feeling of not wanting to touch anybody. It was a beautiful feeling — of purification and spiritual force in my body. I didn't want anybody to touch me, and I didn't want to touch anybody else. I just wanted to hold on to this spirit and not let it get away, not lose it.

I looked around at the stones on the ground and then the grass and the trees and the sky, and everything had an aura. Everything was so beautiful. Even dirt was beautiful. I wanted to take the grass in my hands, and not tear it up; I wanted to touch the tree branches. I realized there was a life force in the rocks, the ground — everything — just like the force in me. Oh, it was a beautiful feeling.

We were invited into the house of one of the women in the community, where a meal had been prepared. I didn't want to eat. So I caught the eye of one of my daughters and gestured towards the door with my head: "I would like to go home." I ate just a few morsels, and then my daughter brought me home. "Please lock the door," I asked her, "and leave me alone." It was summer, and still daylight — around six in the evening. We never lock doors in our community — never. Children run in and out of my house. But, this once, I wanted to be completely alone, without anybody to bother me. I wanted to lie down in peace.

My daughter understood — she had been in the sweatlodge and had the same feeling. So she went home, and I took a shower and lay down on top of my bed. I remember thinking that I wanted to enjoy the spiritual way I felt. Then I slept for ten hours straight. I never sleep that long; normally, I sleep five hours at the most. And when I woke up in the morning, I jumped out of bed. I was ready for the day. Oh, I felt beautiful.

When I was in that sweatlodge, I learned that spiritual force is a two-way thing. You have to have two-way communication. I accepted what I learned and, even now when I am praying, I can see the powerful figure of an eagle, which is a spirit messenger. I believe that the spirit forces are always there, and they are like people, so you can't insult them. You must speak kindly of them and make them happy, just as you must speak well of the dead.

■ ■ ■

> She spoke of paradise
> And angels' guests.
> She spoke of *Niskam*
> And the Holy Spirit.
> She spoke religiously
> Of man's true brotherhood.
> Yet once when she must sit beside me,
> She stood.

I had to learn the hard way about the spiritual side of things. *Kisulkw* (our Creator) is very important to Native people; I learned this from my dad and other people when I was very young. During the time that I was living on all the different reserves, we did not do powwows and the traditional dancing like we do today, but I used to hear Native singing and talking, and Native hymns.

Then, when I went to residential school as a little girl, I was afraid of the priests and nuns who were our teachers. I remember that when I made my first communion, I was petrified; and I didn't know how to confess. I had poor communication skills in English to begin with, and I didn't know what I was supposed to say. I wondered if I should invent things. When you are just a little child, you don't have sins, and here I was expected to confess every week. We children would invent our sins and share them. Oh, it was so ridiculous.

After I came out of residential school when I was sixteen, I did not go near a church for a whole year. I was venting my anger at religion as I had experienced it in the school and then again at the infirmary, which was run by nuns. After that, I did go to church, but on my own time and for my own reasons — for myself. When Frank and I got married, we went to church together. No matter what faults Frank had, he was a church-going person and a spiritual person. For thirty-five years, every morning of our married life, I heard him recite the Prayer to St. Ann. This prayer had been given to Frank before I met him, when he was nineteen and had tuberculosis. He read it over and over until he was free from TB, and then he recited it every day from that time on. Frank made me promise to say the prayer of St. Ann when he died. I keep my promise. Today, every time I recite the prayer, I picture Frank.

We tried to teach our children about religion but also about our Creator and Native spirituality. When I was in my thirties, I began to have unusual experiences — prophetic dreams and other experiences that told me that spiritual forces exist. This is not unusual in our culture; I noticed that one of the friends I often talked to, Julia Stevens, had unusual abilities, like those of a shaman or a *buoin* (a witch). My husband used to call me a *buoin*, too, because I had these strange dreams. At first he would say, "Don't think about that stuff. Don't bother with that foreknowledge stuff in your dreams." But I would still tell him about the dreams and analyze them; after a while he used to tell me, "Well, you're a witch, but you're a good witch!"

> One day my phone rang; my friend was on the line
> We talked awhile, my body tingling down the spine.
> "Are you a *buoin*?" I asked.

"They say that I am, but I am not sure."
"You must be," I said. "My spirit says so."
We talked some more but she would laugh,
"It's surprising how you know."

"Yes," I said, "I can feel something — but not enough."
My friend is gone, but I write this down
To teach about *buoins* — they are still around.

The spiritual part of things — I always kept it alive for myself, deep within my own core. Whatever happened to me, whatever problems I had, I would talk to my Creator in Mi'kmaq. I would converse with *Niskam* (God) when I was alone, just as if I was talking to an individual. "Do you think I'm doing the right thing?" I would ask. "Please give me a sign." I know that sometimes it is impossible to be given a sign, just like it's sometimes impossible for living individuals to give you a sign about what is inside of them. And, of course, the religious part of things and the spiritual part of things don't always solve your problems, either. There were times, when I was a little girl, when I prayed to be delivered from whatever misery I was encountering, and it didn't happen. The misery went on and on and on. And then you have the unhappy realization that religion doesn't always come across for you. But prayer does help. It is possible to receive an answer. Often, when you are in the sweatlodge and you are praying, you get an immediate thought, an answer, right away inside your head.

When this first happened to me, I said, "Gosh, how can this be?" My son Junior and I had a discussion about it and he said, "Well, the sweatlodge was our church before the Europeans came. It is where we pray and where we find our own answers." Anybody else might look at us and say, "Oh, God, what dumb people you are! Are you crazy?" But I do not accept that analysis. I accept my own answers. I wrote a poem about this called "The White Feather." In our culture, the white feather symbolizes compassion, love, healing, wonder, the spirit — all things good.

At Sydney City Hospital, I went to visit a friend.
When I was about to leave, she asked me a favour:
"*Alasutma* (Pray for me)," she said.
I did the best I could — the prayer to St. Ann.
It is the only one I can recite in Micmac.
All the others were quiet.
The next day I had a visitor, my friend's daughter Lottie.
"I had a dream about you," she said.
"You handed me a white feather."

"Your mother will be better," I said,
with an immediate realization of the message.

"*We'la'lin*," I whispered,
"Thank you, my Creator, for the use of my culture
In relaying a message to a loved one."
We'la'lin!

I feel an emptiness where I wish traditional experiences and practice could be part of church activities. I minister the Eucharist in my church, and when I first started the function, I was nervous that I might do something wrong. One day, as I approached the altar, I saw that a dressed feather had been placed on it. The nervousness disappeared and a beautiful peace took its place and I went about my duties at ease. The dressed feather was all it took to put ease in my heart. Just think what would happen if traditional ways were used more often.

I once met a priest who is an Ojibway. I asked him about our cultural beliefs and the white people's church. And he said to me, "Well, that's where I had a problem at one time, when I first became a priest." He didn't fast in the traditional way or do the things that he had done as a young man. Instead, he followed all the rules of the church and put his other ways behind him. But this bothered him. "I still had the feeling that I was supposed to be doing things in my culture, in the traditional ways," he said. "I tried to find answers to the problem, but, no matter who I asked, nobody had answers. I went to my bishop, and he didn't have answers. There was no other Native priest I could talk to at the time. Finally, I went to an elderly individual in my community. She's very wise and very old. And she just said, 'Do what your heart tells you to do.'" So this Ojibway priest followed that advice, and he found his answers in his own tradition.

I like living close to nature
My ancestors did
And being closer to the stars at night
And reading dreams
On interpretation, on what is right.

I like living close to nature
My parents did.
Meeting the sunrise at dawn
Upon seeing the sign of warmth
The sun song

I like living close to nature:
I still do today
Even improvising birchbark for a pot
To cook my meal.
The essence of my being original,
In my instincts.

■ ■ ■

The spiritual part of my culture reminds me to always be on guard. I am both a Christian person and a traditional person. The traditional part is what I was born into; understanding it reminds me whether or not what I am doing is right. Once, I was talking to a young man in Eskasoni. I argued, "Christianity was brought to us in 1610, when the Grand Chief *Mouipeltu* (Membertou) was baptized along with others." The young man's quick reply was, "They may have brought Christianity to us, but we taught spirituality to them." I was surprised by his thinking; but the more I thought about it, the more I was convinced that it may be true.

I have always believed that *Kisulkw* (the Creator) appeared to my people because of their goodness, and that the word *Kisulkip* (the One who made us) was in our Mi'kmaq vocabulary long before anybody "found" us. The fasting, the sweatlodge ceremonies, the dances and songs come from our hearts, and my own experiences convince me in that opinion hourly. Spirituality is a way of life for Natives. It is not a cult or a show. Some of my people are still afraid of it — our brainwashing has been thorough. Myself, I am convinced of its goodness, if it is treated with respect. All spiritual force is positive if you make it that way; if you are fooling around, negativity will result. The Sacred Pipe is still being used, the sweatlodge continues — in all of this, it is the cleansing of the mind and spirit that remains uppermost in my people's minds. We go on from there, to what needs to be done next. Our spiritual tradition was always close to the basics of life for us, the very existence we lived from day to day. I have said time and again that if my people use fasting in a vision quest, maybe it is because, in a vision quest, good spirits give good advice. The sweetgrass burning touches the inner core of one's desire; again, if the intention is good, if the intention is to help others, it will be felt in this ceremony. More and more, people see the powwow as a positive influence. When I dance in the powwow, I feel like a million wonders.

> I am dancing at a *mawiomi*
> My heart is racing at the beat of the drum.
> My happiness holds my body upright
> The beat perceptive to my want.
> I dance for my *Niskam*.
> I have danced since the dawn of time
> My spiritual journey not understood
> Nor my songs, aiming for the sky.
> They do not understand because I put so much thought
> In the supremacy of my *Kisu'lkw*.
> I dance for him
> My joy expressed in the eloquence of my art.
> This is my world,
> The unity told in the holding of hands.
> When others come, they feel the emotion,

They join.
Hence the eagle in the sky when we dance —
He is my messenger
The simple expression righting the balance
I dance
I dance.

■ ■ ■

As you get older, the spiritual becomes more important. You spend more time in that world. In 1991, my third book, *Lnu and Indians We're Called*, was published by Ragweed Press on the 500th anniversary of Columbus' so-called "discovery" of America. I always grow along with my poetry, so in that third book I was even less afraid than before. I analyzed my language and began to voice my thoughts about the spiritual part of my culture.

For example, one day I was sitting down with my daughters and my niece and we brought up the white people's word, "Glooscap." I wrote it down, and then I wrote down the Mi'kmaq word "*Kisulkip*," meaning "the One who created us." And I said, "That's where Glooscap comes from." I think Europeans may have heard Natives saying "*Kisulkip*." To the Natives it meant the supreme spiritual force, and all that is beautiful, and oneness with the land and the animals. I do not think the Christian church is right in teaching that all the Natives who believed in this force before the Europeans came along have gone to a bad place, or limbo, in death.

One time, I was speaking to a group of people in Baddeck, Nova Scotia — some lay people and some nuns and priests. I stood in front of them and I was brave. I said, "Do not sit there and assume we had no spiritual communication with our Creator before the Europeans came. Because, since the dawn of time, since human life was on earth, there have been Native people. And there have been shamans — people who can have a spiritual communication with all life forms. I know people in my own community who see things that other people don't see." And I talked about my own culture and about tolerance. When I had finished, I just said, "This is my gift to you — all that I have talked about." I didn't know what they would do, but I was amazed at myself for saying these things.

People ran up to me and thanked me and hugged me, some of them with tears in their eyes. It was so beautiful, and I didn't feel tired. I felt satisfied. I continue to feel satisfied when I don't hold back honourable words.

> While taking part in a traditional ceremony,
> I felt good.
> When I take part in a Christian ritual,
> I sense the two functions are not that different,
> Sincerity playing a part in both.
> I experience both, I am Micmac,
> The true bond dwelling in my heart,
> Spirituality bridging the two.
>
> The true sense was always with my people,
> Only my rituals were banned.
> Today, the value begins to grow,
> Spark becomes flame.
> I am truly happy,
> The darkness gone.
>
> If you try my core bond,
> You, too, will feel the song.

■ ■ ■

My writing and the craftshop I open in the summer and call *Minuitaqn* (Recreate) have kept me busy in the years since Frank died. I have tried to go on, as productive as possible. Sometimes, one of my children will go with me to speaking engagements, especially if the engagements are not too far away.

In 1991, on the recommendation of the Prime Minister, I was flown to Ottawa to meet the Queen. Before we met her, an aide gave advice on correct protocol — just like the time I received the Order of Canada. I stood before the Queen and waited for her to offer her hand, like we had been told to do; but when she did, everything went out the window. I looked at her and saw that I was looking at another person, one-on-one. That is the Indian way of thinking: The other person is on the same level as you. I experienced a good feeling from the Queen, so I looked her right in the eye and asked, "How are your grandchildren?"

She was flustered because I had broken protocol; I wasn't supposed to ask a question. But in a moment she said, "Oh, they're fine!" in an eager voice. She acted like a grandma. I felt happy after that.

Later, at the reception, people asked me, "What did you say to the Queen that made her smile like that?"

I just told them that I had asked about her grandchildren. It was a good thing to do.

I try not go to too many speaking engagements anymore — just a few nearby. My writing is hampered by Parkinson's Disease, but it does not end. Writing has made my world a goldmine — not through monetary reward, but because I have seen a sea of faces, their eyes glowing with restored honour for our heritage. I know now that the basic reason for my writing and speaking is to bring honour to my people.

Native people are the experts on being poor, we are the experts on recycling, we are even experts on surviving oppression. I have watched when our political leaders — Ovide Mercredi or Elijah Harper — expressed themselves at a sacred dance or prayer, and I have seen the bored faces of non-native politicians. This makes me sad; it seems they could care less what my people do. Our beliefs may be unconventional, but they are what have kept us here; we are here as proof. The reality of five hundred years of control by others is still evident; it still shows through in some places. During a recent Book Festival Week, I spent time in Labrador and saw the sad conditions of the Innu. To my way of perceiving things, it was as if they were like the Mi'kmaq back in the 1940s. When I returned home, I saw one of our leaders on television, his arms raised in a victory sign. My heart skipped a beat as I realized that he didn't know about the conditions at Davis Inlet in Labrador. The money spent on jet bombers flying over the ice in that area would be put to better use helping the people who have occupied this land since time immemorial.

I wish my country would wake up and look more thoroughly at the Native people of today. We have something to offer, in arts, sciences, philosophy; we are not saying, "Gimme, gimme, gimme." The founding fathers of this land we call *Kante'wa'ki* (Canada) were my people, and when they came here it was to live using the best of their knowledge and the utmost perseverance. We were the first explorers, but had no thought of glory, monetary reward or conquest. We survived. Yet, the world hears the cry of the conquerers as they are immortalized time and time again; society ignores the beauty of our culture. Native people today are still like strangers in our own land.

What I would like to ask now is that you look at my people without the negative image, and listen to our voices — our wampum, our stone writings, our words. Analyze, if you wish, but listen.

■ ■ ■

More and more, I compose songs now. I may be sitting down in my kitchen or walking around or cooking, and I begin to hum. Then I get a pen and write something down and it comes out as a song. The songs and poetry are spontaneous; I never know when inspiration will occur.

I was a songwriter even before I became a poet. From the time I was a little girl I was what you would call a hummer. Melodies would roll around in my head; I wouldn't know if I had picked them up from hymns, the roll of an incoming wave or wind sounds. I was shy, though, so the songs were put away and I only sang when I was speaking at a school or a gathering.

During the Oka Crisis in the summer of 1990, I was very affected by the incidents that were happening in my country. The whole time, I was thinking, "How can they be doing this to us in our country? It's like civil war." My reaction was to create the "Oka Poem" and the "Oka Song." I wrote the verses from the Native viewpoint, attempting to touch my audience and their heartstrings. Usually, when I am speaking to an audience about this incident, I point out the inconsistent attitudes of non-Natives towards what happened at the time, then end my speech with the "Oka Song." Many times, I have received a standing ovation. I always try to move my audience in poetry and song, making fun of myself at times, but emphasizing that we are a wronged nation by using what I have learned from my cultural background.

The "Oka Song" became a popular, often-requested melody — today, it is even being sung in Mohawk. In the summer of 1991, I thought I had better find someone to transcribe it onto a songsheet. The first person I asked was Elizabeth Cremo, the daughter of the famous fiddle champion, Lee Cremo, who is from Eskasoni. She told me about Professor Gordon Smith from Queen's University in Ontario, who was working with Lee at the time. A little while later, a white-haired man walked up to me near my craftshop and asked if I was Rita Joe and if I wished to have a song transcribed onto a songsheet. "How in the world did you know?" I asked; I had told only Elizabeth about this desire. The man explained that he was Gordon Smith. He browsed in the craftshop while I recorded a tape of my song.

Gordon Smith took my song and my typed-out page of words, and returned in a day or two with a songsheet. My reaction was disbelief, in English and Mi'kmaq! "Oh, you work fast," I told him. I was amazed to see my song done up in a professional manner, and felt happy realizing the result of my simple creativity. I thought to myself that if a song got published, the music would show what I have always been trying to show — the teachings and value of my culture, our hope that we can rebuild our loss of spirit. Gordon asked if he could take my songs to his students at the university. I taped a dozen or so songs for him in my old woman voice, hoping that the students would understand the words. I still could not believe this turn of events.

Around Christmas of 1991, Gordon sent me a tape of one of his students, Kevin Alstrup, singing my songs with guitar accompaniment. I couldn't contain my happiness, and when my son-in-law, Tom Sylliboy, walked into the house, I said to him, "Listen to this Tom! See how good my songs sound when someone else is singing!" Tom listened carefully. I was looking for a reaction from him because he is a professional musician and singer, and because he is one of my people. Needless to say, Tom was very enthusiastic.

In the summer of 1993, Kevin Alstrup came to Cape Breton and stayed with us in Eskasoni for several months. I got along well with Kevin; he is easy to please. He ate without complaint what we Natives call "cultural food" — four cents cake (fried bread), and all the rest of it. We would sing my songs together, and he would transcribe them later at the craftshop, where he was staying. I learned later that sometimes he transcribed them by candlelight, as he did not like the smell of the kerosene from the lamp in the shop. At times, Kevin went to visit a friend who was a basket-maker, and he eventually learned how to make baskets; at other times, he developed friendships on the reserve. We worked that way through the fall, until he returned home.

One of the songs Kevin and I worked on was a Christmas song, "And Then We Heard the Baby Cry." One day we were in my kitchen working; Kevin was strumming the tune, and I suddenly had a beautiful feeling inside, like a ripple on my chest wall, creating a tingle of goodness. "Oh!" I said out loud.

"What's wrong?" Kevin asked, eyes as big as saucers.

"Oh, it's nothing," I said. "I think the guy we are singing about likes our song."

Around Christmas, the Eskasoni Church choir heard "And Then We Heard the Baby Cry," and developed an interest in it. When it was sung in the church at midnight mass on Christmas Eve, my tears fell, but they tasted sweet. I listened to my song with my head down, afraid to look at the choir members. The spiritual, emotional feeling inside me made me tremor with Parkinson's Disease. "*Niskam* (God)," I thought, "I am so happy to be able to create something for you." The clapping of my people after the mass was music to my ears. The appreciation of my own people means a lot to me.

■ ■ ■

Frank and Ann at Frank's graduation from university in 1984.

Me with Bernadette *(left)* and Ann in 1987.

Me as I appeared at many readings, in my traditional dress.

Me and Carla Jean (Caroline's daughter) in 1988.

A family Christmas in the late 1980s. *First row (left to right):* Frank, me, Ann. *Behind me:* Step, Frances, Caroline. *Back row:* Basil, Phyllis, Junior, Dana (foster child) with Sherry (Bernadette's daughter). Bernadette with son Brad, Richard and Stephen (Bernadette's sons), John Denny (Frances' son) and Ann Thomas (Frances' daughter).

Frank in my craftshop in August 1989, one week before he died.

I found this photo of me in my husband's wallet when he died. Frank took it at Oka.

A photo from 1990, when I received the Order of Canada from Governor General Ray Hnatyshyn *(right)*.

Me in the gym in Eskasoni in 1993, at the launch of a film about my life and poetry. The film-maker, Brian Guns, is beside me *(right)*.

A photo of me meeting the Queen in 1993.

Me, Prime Minister Brian Mulroney and Caroline, after meeting the Queen.

Me with Phyllis and Nathan (Step's son) in the early 1990s.

Me in my craftshop, *Minitaqn*, in the 1990s.

Me in 1996 with Caroline's son Frankie Joe *(right back)*, Caroline *(left back)* and her daughters Carla Jean *(left)* and Fallon *(right)*.

Me in 1993, after receiving an Honourary Doctor of Laws from Dalhousie University.

Recently, I was holding my little grandson Frankie Joe. I gave thanks that I could still hold him, my thoughts on my husband; the grandson is named after Frank. "Frankie Joe, Frankie Joe," I kept repeating. "I love you." Sometimes I am full of wonder, because I am so blessed with a loving family. *We'la'lin Sesos we'la'lin* (Thank you, Jesus, I thank you). My love overflows for my children and twenty-two grandchildren.

My eldest daughter Phyllis is a beautiful person, artistic, strong and spiritual. I often compare our lives; she is so strong, even after many hardships. Last year, after we had gone away together for six days, we returned to find that Phyllis' house had burned down. She ran inside my home, grabbing her head and asking, "What about my children?"

"They are okay," Junior told her.

She was trembling so much. I hugged her. "Your children are okay."

Phyllis now lives in the craftshop, which we fixed up until a house can be provided; three of her children are with her. Phyllis and I have long talks on every subject we can think of. In the early days of her marriage, she experienced abuse, so she spent time working out with barbells; she could throw punches like a pro. She is without a husband today, but has four boys and one daughter. My granddaughter is often told she is like me; this makes me feel good. One of Phyllis' sons is married, so soon I may be a great-grandmother.

After Step picked up the pieces of her broken marriage and went to Teachers College, she worked as a substitute teacher and taught Native crafts. She does this today and is happy. Sometimes she talks about her father's encouraging words; he was always telling her she should upgrade her level of education. She still thinks about doing this.

Junior (as everybody calls Francis) is an easygoing individual, more like me than his father. He lets the ups and downs he encounters in life just slide off, and goes on from there. The traditional part of his life is important to him; he welcomes his spirituality and uses it to ask for help for his people. When he has confusion about the spiritual part of things, we talk about it. He does everything he can to help me in my writing and songs, and if anything creates a problem for me, he tries to correct it. I have a good rapport with Junior — although I have no control over what he does — and I have a better understanding of the unseen forces because of him. The poem I call "Dancing Eagle" is about his vision. It was so beautiful, I had to tell it, but other than that I do not tell his stories. If he wishes to share his stories, it is up to him. He has not yet found the right person to spend his life with, but I do not worry about him. He is a good man, and he is good to me.

Basil is another happy-go-lucky person, but he is also strong-willed and ambitious, more like his father than me. He is not married but I don't worry about him; I know he can hold his own and will do his best.

Frances married in her teens and has two boys and a girl. She has a good husband, Tom, who is a Councillor and a musician. Frances is now going to college and we have long talks while driving to bingo or town. Her children are like her, with Tom's firm but kind attitude.

Caroline married a man we did not know, and later we found out that she was in an abusive situation. We told her that she must help herself, and she did that. Today she lives in Eskasoni with her three children. She is a gifted craftsperson; people say that she has golden fingers.

The youngest of my children, Ann, is mostly at home with me. She was going to Saint Mary's University when her dad died, but then she lost interest as she grieved. She had only two credits to go before she finished her B.A., but I did not push her to do so; she was too sad. Today, she has plans to work on finishing it. I like having my daughter live with me. She is funny, sensitive, kind of shy but still the *mta'ksn* (baby) to the rest of the family.

■ ■ ■

These words were written by my third daughter, Bernadette, who died on April 4, 1992, at thirty-two years of age:

I am a battered wife
The hurt is so much inside, my spirit is down.
I go to sleep, a prayer in my mind.
In my dream I see an injured man on a cot, so pitiful.
There are tears running down his face.
I wipe them away, moving closer.
He is familiar, the bearded face, so gentle and kind.
I wiped his tears away, thinking to myself
I wiped his tears away, suddenly comforted.

The next day I tell my mother
"You know who it was," she said.
"You were at the bottom of the barrel, He came."
I look at myself differently now
I am one of His creations, acceptable
A receiver of a message.
Today I am free of the abuser, just being myself
And in my mind, I wiped the tears away
I will always have that gift
I wiped the tears away.

Bernadette had a stormy marriage after falling in love when she was a teenager. There were good times and bad times; her four children were her life. While Frank was alive, he and I just saw the surface of her life with her family. She did not confide all the problems until the time of her father's death, and her marriage went down then. She did not have time to grieve for her father. I hugged her a lot when she came to see me; she could not hide her sad eyes. I loved her so much, but I could not control what happened to her. Her disappointments in life just broke her heart.

This poem was also written by Bernadette:

When I was a little girl, something was taken from me,
Something precious, that all females consider a treasure.
And all through the years, from child to woman,
A nagging thought was pushed to the back of the mind,
A hurt so great that few of us know;

We tend to shut it out, suppress or bind.
When I became a woman, it was still there,
Abuse from others brought it out, laid it bare,
Until one day I met a learned man;
He told me this, I keep it always on my mind:
"If something dear is taken from you when you are a child
It is replaced with something more precious,
More priceless than this world will ever know."
I have this special gift that few of us know,
A gift so strange, so unusual,
I am afraid sometimes. It is like my shadow.

There are no words to describe my feelings when Bernadette died. She had promised to come see me that Sunday, to play cards and eat my elegant dinner. I still can hear the joking, loving way she spoke to me on the phone.

All my family loved Bernadette. Frances and Bernadette were closest to each other, and it hit Frances the hardest when she died. Frances dreamt about her constantly, and in one dream she asked, "Are you with Dad?"

Bernadette answered, "Yes."

After Bernadette died, I included one of her poems with my own writing in an anthology of stories by Native women. Her husband, Stephen, called me up afterwards and said, "I just read the poem that Bernadette wrote. You have some nerve putting that in a book. I thought you always worked on a positive level." He was angry because he had been named an abuser.

I replied, "I am working on a positive level. That poem happens to work for other people. When Bernadette wrote it, she was using writing as therapy. It's the same with me. Almost all my married life, I used writing as therapy." We had a big argument.

Later, I told my daughter Ann about the phone call. And she said, "Don't remove my sister's voice. That's what Stephen is trying to do — erase her. She was my sister and I loved her. We all loved her and this is her voice. It's a voice from the grave, but it's a voice."

So I told Bernadette's husband: "The truth hurts, but I will not erase her."

I know now that love cannot be erased. A long time ago, my dad left that impression with me; the warmth I remember from my mother reinforced it. Because I know that, I have recently been able to heal the animosity that I carried for Stephen. On Christmas Day, two of my sons, a grandson and I went to his house in East Bay. I had a long talk with him, and listened to him; finally we hugged to heal our differences.

Bernadette's children are my life today. There are three boys and one girl; I always search their faces for some feature of hers. My expressions of love spill over for them.

> She is silent but her word is there
> She lies in the ground
> We, her family in sorrow,
> Just memory bound.
> She is silent, but her image speaks
> In our dreams she comes
> Sometimes low or laughing.
> She is silent but her hopes are there
> Tomorrow they may be realized
> They cannot be quieted.
>
> Now they linger in my mind.
> Why did she go?

■ ■ ■

Many years ago, I gave Bernadette the nickname "omely," a loving term combining "homely" with an Indian sound. I remember one day, when she was little, she came running in to me on her long legs, with a pout on her face. "I know the meaning of the word now! I looked it up in a dictionary."

A wave of emotion swept over me as I swooped her up and hugged her. "I love you, Tuce. I love you with all of my heart."

The image of her running to me, the hug and the words, are always in my mind. I love you, my beautiful Bernadette. I love you.

• • •

Now, my life from day to day is just "one at a time." Often I wake early in the morning. This is my best time for creating. If the sun is out, I do the early morning sunrise ceremony; if it isn't out, I say a prayer in English. The turnaround comes easy for me; *Kisulkip* (the One who created us) hears, no matter what language we use.

> In a very early dawn, I am awake and do not know why
> To a room in the East I enter, and look at the sky.
> There is a glow at the edge of heaven and earth.
> I realize I must communicate with *Niskam*
> A fire must be lit that is our way
> I light a candle and to the spirit I pray.
> In immediate time, the visions come,
> In dances and song and the pound of the drums.
> An amazement is contained in my native mind
> What is most beautiful the senses find.
> The humility speaks loud and clear,
> My culture, put down so long, now dear.

I sometimes write for hours, typing with one finger because my left hand is disabled from the Parkinson's Disease. My mind still works wonders, though. I write mostly to inspire others; I think that if others look at me — blind in one eye, almost deaf, often with socks that don't match — the attitude I put forth may convince them that they could do even better.

When I was presented with an Honourary Doctor of Laws from Dalhousie University in 1993, this is what I told the people there. The stories come from my heart, like a song I am continually singing, searching for a way to move you. When I began to write, I wondered why the beauty of my people had not been recorded. Then my research led me to the petroglyphs, the wampum, the hieroglyphs. Understanding came to me in dreams. It did not matter to me if I was considered odd, mysterious or just hard to understand; I blurted out everything I felt needed to be told, baring the innermost secrets of my culture, using myself like a book with no cover. My continuing aria created in me a spiritual sensitivity. I enjoyed feeling this, and nothing fazed me anymore. Today I know that some of my words have reached people; in 1996, a Dutch composer even made a symphony from my work. I am glad to be here, to know that my words might have helped somebody, no matter what their culture. *Keskowle'ap, nikay ila'si* (My load was heavy, but now I feel good).

The spiritual part of my life is beautiful. This past Christmas Eve, I went to mass at Eskasoni Church and saw that the place was full, with teenagers as well as adults; I was surprised and glad to see the teenagers. The Christmas songs were sung in English and Mi'kmaq and the homey atmosphere of the church filled my heart with love. I sat there calm, my tired body full of small trembles. During the early part of the service, our priest spoke in Mi'kmaq — a full page of our language; we were so surprised that we clapped. The attempts of the priests and the nuns in the choir to speak our language always moves me. I thank them every time they do it. At the end of the service, the familiar twang of the guitar moved my heart; it was my song they were singing. My body trembled and I pressed my palms flat and held them between my knees, hoping no one would notice my emotion.

After I return home from church most Sundays, my satisfaction is in cooking a good meal. The rest of the week my meals are mostly hash-a-wey or just fast lunches, but on Sunday I cook a full course meal. Family members like coming on Sunday; they come all the time, but on Sunday they know there is sure to be something good to eat.

I am an elder in the community, and it feels good to be respected and admired. Even today, I would not trade the best place in the city for the home I now have on the reserve. Many of the elderly people are my friends, and the younger crowd — as I call everyone who is even a year younger than me — are always visiting. Helen Sylliboy and her three sisters visit, and on Sunday, after church and the family meal, a group of women come over. We play cards, gossip, compare recipes, trade secrets, joke and talk about everything happening in the community. There is nobody in Eskasoni who is an enemy; I love people, and the love bounces back.

I have a good feeling in my heart about our accomplishments. I admire the achievements of people like Mary Rose Julian, who works on the Native curriculum in the schools, and teachers like Eleanor Bernard, Elizabeth Paul Ryan and Gale Doucette Stevens, who pass on the learning to their students. My daughter Step works in the same area, teaching crafts and substituting for other teachers. All of them are proud of the Native Curriculum Centre they have established.

Recently, the Mi'kmaq *Kina'masuti* (Process of Learning) Conference was held at our school gym. A lot of people passed on their concerns about the transfer of jurisdiction for education from the federal government to the Nova Scotia Mi'kmaq communities. The transfer is not yet in production, but the concerns must be addressed. They were heard by the *Saqmows* (Chiefs) of the Maritimes, by the Indian Affairs officials and by other professionals. I felt so good that we are doing this. I sum up my feelings about the transfer of jurisdiction in these words: *"Kisa'tue'k tan ke'tulukatmekp aqq wela'sikek* (We did what we had to do, and we did it well)."

> This morning, I saw a film
> About my people, the Micmac.
> There was Sarah Denny singing a lullaby
> Her son Joel looking on.
> Murdena Marshall was speaking about our culture
> The basic knowledge she wants to teach.
> I sat there feeling good, seeing children walk around,
> Their dancing to a song, goodness knows for how long.
> My heart warmed inside, seeing Noel and Jean Doucette,
> The homey atmosphere, all families taking part.
> O yes, I feel good inside.
> Today they show the facts of life: that Micmacs take pride.
> I feel good, I'm growing old
> I always knew the good,
> I often told.

My life is in Eskasoni, with my friends and my children and grandchildren. The more my grandchildren come to visit, the more I love them. And it is not only my own grandchildren — all the children call me grandma. Even older people call me "*Su'kwis* (Auntie)." I love that. Who could ask for more? Being a survivor has made me build a brave heart — what we would call a *kinap*. Our tradition tells of the men who are *kinaps*, but I think there must be women *kinaps*, too. I leave behind the memory of an orphan child, picking herself up from the misery of being nobody, moving little grains of sand until she could talk about the first nations of the land.

> I have named my craftshop *Minuitaqn*
> Meaning, "To recreate."
> "To recreate what?" you say.
> The crafts of my people, the Micmac
> Inspiration swells in their heart
> Ready to be fired by need
> Then it flowers
> There you see minuitaqn.
> The creation is in their hands
> It is native, and it is ours.

■ ■ ■

A few years ago, I was invited to the Museum of Civilization in Ottawa. They asked me to speak on July 2 — the day after Canada Day. So, when I spoke, I asked, "Why have I been asked to speak in second place, on the day after Canada Day? Who is more Canadian than I am?"

Later, I mingled with people at the museum and I came across a drum. It was under glass and it was very old — hundreds and hundreds of years old — but I could see it had Indian symbols on it. So I stood in front of that drum in my Native dress and tried to discover who had owned it. I was standing there and standing there for the longest time, concentrating, trying to visualize, not speaking to anybody else. Finally, I began to get an image. I could see a figure, and in my mind I was trying to bring into focus the features of the person sitting in front of the drum. Just then, a man — a non-native — interrupted me and said, "Are you trying to find out who owned the drum?"

I looked up at him and said, "Yes."

He said, "I've been watching you. You've been standing there for nearly an hour."

"I'm a Native," I explained, "and the spirit of the individual who owned that drum may try to communicate with me."

"I tried before you came," he replied.

So I asked him, "Well, who owned the drum then?"

"A Native, of course," he laughed.

"A Native!" I said. "Could you see the features of the Native?"

"No," he replied. "It's as if they were out of focus. You can see the outline of someone playing the drum, but you cannot see his face."

This is what it is like for the Native people of today. It is hard for you to see our face, and sometimes it is even hard for us to see ourselves. In the first poem in my first book, I wrote:

> I am the Indian,
> And the burden
> Lies yet with me.

Twenty years later, I am thinking the same thing. The brave part is in taking on history and leaving your own story. Today I still say, "This is who I am. I want to share it with you." *Ta'ho'*! (So be it.)

> I am just an Indian on this land
> I am sad, my culture you do not understand.
> I am just an Indian to you now
> You wrinkle your brow.

Today you greet me with bagpipes
Today you sing your song to me
Today we shake hands and see
How we keep good company.
Today I will tell stories
Today I will play the drum and dance
Today I will say what is on my mind
For being friends is our goal.
Today I will show you I am just like you
Today I will show what is true
Today I will show we can be friends
Together we agree.
Today I will tell you about my race
Today I will share what is mine
Today I will give you my heart
This is all we own
Today I show.
Hello everybody, my name is Rita Joe.

APPENDIX 1

Six Songs

Compiled and transcribed by Gordon E. Smith
Comments by Rita Joe

A Note on the Transcriptions:

The musical transcriptions of Rita Joe's songs are meant as "blueprints" or guidelines rather than definitive performing versions. They are entry points for anyone — teachers, children, adults — interested in bridging gaps and breaking barriers within and between cultures through the use of words and music.

In compiling these songs, Kevin Alstrup and I were concerned to retain respect for the words, since we knew that Rita's message (her educational intent, in the broadest sense) would be conveyed inevitably through the poetry. For Rita, these pieces are "sung poems" about her people. For Kevin and I — outsiders — they represent a multi-layered challenge. The process of rendering them in musical notation raises issues about transcription and representation — issues which we explore in greater depth in an article entitled, "Words and Music of Micmac Poet Rita Joe: Dialogic Ethnomusicology" (*Canadian Folk Music Journal*, 1995). The songs published here are part of a larger, ongoing project to research and transcribe Rita's songs, and this process has led us to a deeper understanding and appreciation of Mi'kmaq thinking and creativity, as well as a greater awareness of social, cultural and political issues. The work has required dialogue among three individuals of divergent backgrounds and viewpoints (Kevin Alstrup, myself and, of course, Rita) and this has led each of us to new knowledge of the "other."

— Gordon E. Smith,
Queen's University, Department of Music,
1996

1. Oka Song

The Oka crisis in Quebec affected me in a contradictory way because I was thinking, "This is my country!" yet my country was doing things I never for a moment thought they would do to my people. I know there are two sides to any story, but I have to side with my people here. I think that if the situation were reversed, any cultural group in this land would have acted upon the same grievance. I just try to point out the pain the Oka crisis caused. The Mi'kmaq sided readily with the Mohawks, to defend a cause. The majority on the other side also did what they thought was right. The aftermath: no solution at all. As I see it, our hands are always tied. We give in because the little ant cannot fight the elephant. Our only way is to win your heart. We cannot hide the sadness in our eyes; our hand is still offered — please take it and be friends. This is Canada, and unity is needed by all of us.

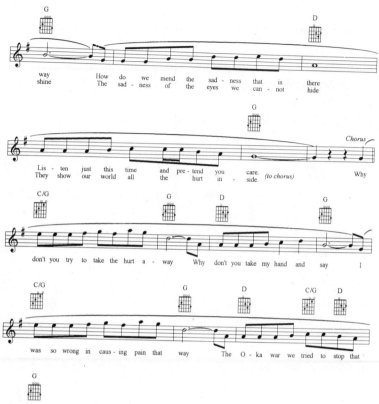

way
shine
How do we mend the sad - ness that is there
The sad - ness of the eyes we can - not hide

Lis - ten just this time and pre - tend you care. *(to chorus)*
They show our world all the hurt in - side.

Chorus
Why

don't you try to take the hurt a - way Why don't you take my hand and say I

was so wrong in caus - ing pain that way The O - ka war we tried to stop that

day.

2. Five Hundred Years

I am a Native person struggling with the thought of the so-called "discovery" of my people, and I envisage the event differently from the non-native. Our reception of the non-natives was in good faith. We still feel the effects of our offer of the land, and the humiliation of Aboriginals continues today, just as it has at any given time of contact with non-natives. Five hundred years is a long time for us to bend to your wishes. Look at us as we look at you, one on one — the Aboriginal mind works that way, and depends on the great support of friends. Five hundred years is a long time to take to learn that we are not the bad ones in this story. The road of tears must end somewhere. Honour lies just beyond reach; accept me as I am, not as what you want me to be.

help your kin / My learn-ing there / I showed the hum-ble way.
hun-dred years / My learn-ing there / I showed the hum-ble way.
know the song / The giv-en time, / we show the hum-ble way.

You tried to see / but held by hid-den tale / Five hun-dred years,
Don't let me down, / let us try, try a-gain / Five hun-dred years,
Don't let me down, / let us try, try a-gain / Five hun-dred years,

we long to know the mem-o-ry. (to chorus) Dear Ca-na-da I
the hon-our there don't let it fade. (to chorus)
the hon-our there we gain as one. (to coda)

Chorus

cried the road of tears try-ing to show my life we al-ways care

Five hun-dred years is a long and lone-ly way Stran-gers we

are why don't you see we are the same. (to next verse)

Coda

Five hun-dred years, the hon-our there we gain as one.

3. Don't Turn Away

"Don't Turn Away" speaks for itself. The thought behind it is that when our loved ones turn to us for comfort, we turn away from them. What makes us turn away is the tiring part of caring for an alcoholic. Their promises are always made and broken. We are let down so often, we turn away when they are made. I speak directly to the illness: The end is not pretty. Hope is there if we listen. The glamour is a fading image; there is no middle road. We must face reality, not sweep it under the rug or make believe that we are doing something when nothing is happening. The caring part comes when we listen one more time, because we love the individual. The emotion that is in all of us is the most powerful medicine we can use.

1. I wear a smile when I spend the time of drink-ing   I play the
3. Come stay with me, I will be your friend for - ev - er   Come play with
4. So hold me now, the world is slow - ly fad- ing   The lights are

field for some-where joy is here   The time goes on and I'm a-fraid it's
me, don't turn a - way a - gain   I'm so a - lone, my heart is slow-ly
dim, the bells are all a - round.   Your rea-sons there, I'll lis - ten if you

stop - ping   come stay with me, don't you turn a-way a - gain.
break - ing   I'll be your friend, if you help me once a - gain.   (to chorus)
tell them   I'll be your friend, if you help me once a - gain.

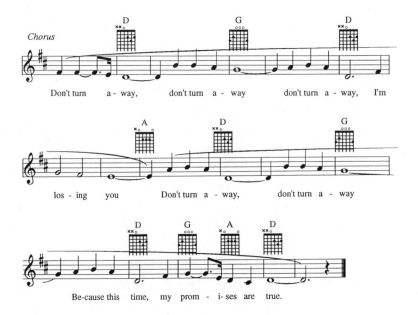

Chorus

Don't turn a - way, don't turn a - way don't turn a - way, I'm los - ing you Don't turn a - way, don't turn a - way Be-cause this time, my prom - i- ses are true.

Verse 2 (spoken without accompaniment)

It bothers me, when drug abuse and booze are killing me. It bothers me, when there's no one else around. Why do they leave? They stayed when there was drinking. Why do they leave when all of my money is gone?

4. Two Roads

When I wrote the song "Two Roads," I was thinking of our Native youth. The road is harder for them — they have peer pressure, trying to be one of the crowd, but always trying to follow the right path as well. Our youth are like the flowers we plant — we nurture them and watch to see how the plant is doing. We try to coax it into a good flowering, always helping it along. We only hope they take the good road. It is hard, but worth it — especially for the happiness at the end.

1. Two roads we go, there's no one else a - round Two roads we
2. Two roads we go, there's no one else a - round Two roads we
3. Two roads we go, there's no one else a - round Two roads we

tra - vel, til hap - pi - ness we find. And when we find it, we
tra - vel, the most we look to find. And some-times no-where, the
tra - vel, the good and some-times wrong. And if we find it, we

try with all our heart To make the most of
an - swer we don't find It hurts to lose on
try with all our heart Give hap - pi - ness to

ev' - ry - thing Two roads we try to win the game. (to spoken vs. 1)
ev' - ry - thing Two roads not al - ways there to win. (to spoken vs. 2)
o - - thers Two roads we tried, we won the game.

(spoken verses)

Verse 1
Each one of us travel on two roads,
Sometimes they are good sometimes they are bad.
But whatever road we eventually take
we are the ones who decide.
Sometimes obstacles fall along the way
we try to avoid them,
Sometimes weaknesses take a stranglehold, we work harder.

Verse 2
So the road which determines our value
is usually the one with the briar patch,
the hard road proving to ourselves we have
what it takes to be a success.

5. And Then We Heard A Baby Cry

On a Christmas show, I heard beautiful songs
My heart felt good; I began to hum
I began to write words, humming along
Very soon it was a pretty song.

A professor from Queen's University
Arrived at my door.
We talked about songs to transcribe
One of my Christmas songs was done
Very soon, it was sung
By the Eskasoni Church Choir.

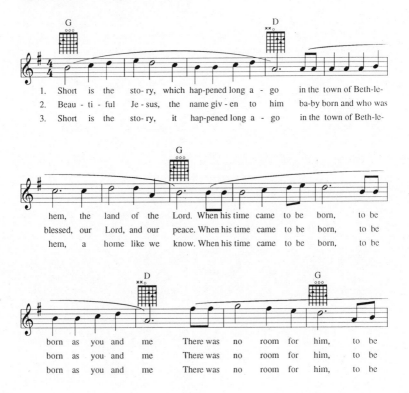

1. Short is the sto- ry, which hap-pened long a - go in the town of Beth-le-
2. Beau - ti - ful Je - sus, the name giv - en to him ba-by born and who was
3. Short is the sto- ry, it hap-pened long a - go in the town of Beth-le-

hem, the land of the Lord. When his time came to be born, to be
blessed, our Lord, and our peace. When his time came to be born, to be
hem, a home like we know. When his time came to be born, to be

born as you and me There was no room for him, to be
born as you and me There was no room for him, to be
born as you and me There was no room for him, to be

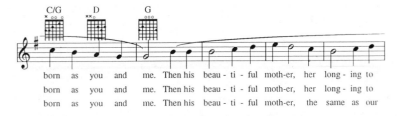

born | as | you | and | me. | Then his | beau - ti - ful | moth-er, | her | long - ing to
born | as | you | and | me. | Then his | beau - ti - ful | moth-er, | her | long - ing to
born | as | you | and | me. | Then his | beau - ti - ful | moth-er, | the | same as our

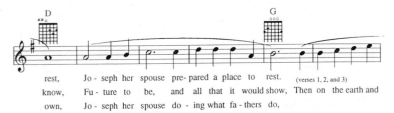

rest, | Jo - seph her | spouse | pre- pared a | place to | rest. | (verses 1, 2, and 3)
know, | Fu - ture to | be, | and all that it | would show, | Then on the earth and
own, | Jo - seph her | spouse | do - ing what fa - thers do,

in the sky, | the time stood still, the | time stood still, | and

then we heard a ba- by cry, | a ba- by cry, a | ba- by cry. | And

then we heard a ba- by cry, | a ba- by cry, a | ba- by cry.

6. Micmac Honour Song

The words to the Micmac Honour Song came to George Paul of Red Bank, New Brunswick, during a sweatlodge. The melody was already on his mind and the words appeared when he was feeling spiritual harmony during the sweat. The song is sacred to the Mi'kmaq because of how it came to be. It can be sung by any culture, though; the words are for every nation. They tell of coming together to help one another when the need arises. The Native words in translation are as follows: "Let us honour our ancestry and help each other, as our Creator has put us on this earth to do." Those words say it all.

The Micmac Honour Song is a prayer in a chant. It usually helps the person who is singing it and the people nearby who hear it. I wanted to share the song with all nations so I asked George Paul for permission to use it in my book. I am fortunate that he said, "Yes."

Note from Gordon E. Smith: The transcription of the Micmac Honour Song is based on a tape recording of the song by Joel Denny (Eskasoni). I am grateful to Joel, and also to Bernie Francis (Sydney, Nova Scotia) for his kind assistance with the Mi'kmaq text.

(translation)

Let us highly respect our people
My dear friends let us come together
Let us highly respect our origin
My dear friends let us help one another
Let us help one another according to the Creator's intentions as to
    why he placed us here.

APPENDIX 2

Glossary of Mi'kmaq Words and Phrases

A'wi = Louis

Aklasiew = white people

Aklasiewto't = white person beaten

Aknutm te' sik kejitu = I tell what I know

Alasutma = Pray for me

Alasutmay ujit kilow = I pray for you

Api = bow

App kinu'tmui = Teach me again

Aqamoq = white ash

Bad womani'sk = unmarried, "experienced" woman

Buoin = witch

E'e = Yes

E'e, kesalipni'k na = Yes, they loved me

Epit = middle aged woman

Epite's = young woman

Epitejij = girl

'Iknmulek na! = We give! Let us give!

Inua'kis = to be Indian

Ji'nm nemi'k = I see a man

Jika'winen we'jitutqsip kutoy ninen = Look at us and you, too, will find the good

Jiktek = All is still

Kante'wa'ki = Canada

Ke'salu'kik aqq kesaluksi'kik = We love them and they love us

Ke'snukay = I am sick

Kejitu mu telianukw katu welte'tm = I know it is not true but I am happy

Kekin a'matin kewe'l = tools for learning

Keskowle'ap, nikay ila'si = My load was heavy, but now I feel good

Ki'l ktla taqn! = It is your fault!

Ki'su'lk weswalata = Our Creator took him

Kijinu = Grandmother

Kiju' = Mother

Kikwesu = muskrat

Kikwesu'sk = muskrat root

Kina'masuti = process of learning

Kinap = brave heart

Kisa'tue'k tan ke'tulukatmekp aqq wela'sikek = We did what we had to do, and we did it well

Kisikuisk = Old Woman

Kisulkip = the One who made us

Ki'su'lk/Kisu'lk/Kisulkw = the Creator; the Great Spirit

Ki'su'lk weswalata = Our Creator took him

Kji-Saqamow = Great Chief

Kogo'ey wejinkalin' = Why did you leave me?

Kujinu = Grandfather

Kwitn = canoe

Lnu = Native person

Lnui'simk = Indian talk

Maja'sit = she goes

Maskwi = birch

Mawiomi = powwow

Me'tasimon = You smell romantic

Mejukat = who defecates

Mikjij = turtle

Minuitaqn = recreate

Misekn = Rags

Menaqa tlitue'n = Act correctly

Moqnja'tu'wi' = putting the sugar on things

Mouiemto'q a'la'nej = O come let us adore him

Mouipeltu = Membertou

Mta'ksn = baby

Mu wela'luksiwun = You have no gratitude

Muk atukoiew = Do not speak of legends

Muk kwe'ji li'ewij = Do not let your sister go

Mussy mon eta = Mi'kmaq insult

Na ni'n Ni'kmawa'j = I am a Mi'kmaq

Na'taqma'si = Go ashore

Nekm = her, him, them

Nemi'k = I see

Nenwite'ten ke'luk weji tu'ap = Remember: I found the good

Niskam = God

Niskam apoqnmui' = God help me

Nmis = sister

Ntapekiaqn = my song

Nutaq = I hear

Pi'tow'ke = upriver

Pi'tow'ke'waq na nin = I am/We are from upriver

Pla'n = Francis

Po'tlo'tek = Chapel Island

Ro'kewte'likan = crooked buying

Salite' = funeral auction

Saqmows = Chiefs

Siknoqkwa tasi = I am tired of hearing myself

Sitnaqn = orphan(s)

Sitnaqn na = She is an orphan

Snawey = rock maple

Su'kwis = Auntie

Ta'ho' = So be it

Taqmku'k = Newfoundland

Teken = Which?

Tepknuset = moon; month

Tesipojij = workhorse bench

Tewa'lud = Taken Out

We'kopa'q = Whycocomagh; the end of water

We'la'lin = thank you

We'la'lin Sesos we'la'lin = Thank you, Jesus, I thank you

Wena = Who?

Wkwejij = sister

Yi-ya = Does it hurt?

Mi'kmaq lament for the dead:

Ma'lta elasnl Se'susil
Saqamaw, wula l'mu'sipn,
Mu pa npisoqq wijikitiekaq,
Skatu kejitu nike',
Kisu'lk iknimultal msit ta'n tel-tamjil

Martha said to Jesus:
Lord, if you had been here
My brother would not have died,
But I know that even now
God will give you whatever you ask
of him

APPENDIX 3

Poems from the Text *(in order of appearance)*

Abbreviations:
PRJ = *Poems of Rita Joe* (Abanaki Press, 1978, out of print)
SE = *Song of Eskasoni: More Poems of Rita Joe* (Ragweed Press, 1988)
LIWC = *Lnu and Indians We're Called* (Ragweed Press, 1991)

APPENDIX 4

Select Bibliography

Books:

Joe, Rita. *Lnu and Indians We're Called*. Charlottetown, PEI: Ragweed Press, 1991.

Joe, Rita. *Poems of Rita Joe*. Halifax, NS: Abanaki Press, 1978.

Joe, Rita. *Song of Eskasoni: More Poems of Rita Joe*. Charlottetown, PEI: Ragweed Press, 1988.

Articles:

Joe, Rita. "The Gentle War." *Canadian Woman Studies/les cahiers de la femme* 10, 2&3 (Summer/Fall 1989). pp. 27-9.

Joe, Rita. "Here and There in Eskasoni." Regular column in *Micmac News* (1969-73).

Joe, Rita. "Honour Song of the Micmac," in *Kelusultiek: Original Women's Voices of Atlantic Canada*. Halifax, NS: Institute for the Study of Women, Mount Saint Vincent University, 1994. pp. 18-62.

Joe, Rita. "The Legend of Mud-lane," in *Another Night: Cape Breton Stories True & Short & Tall*. Ronald Caplan (ed.). Cape Breton, NS: Breton Books. 1994.

Joe, Rita. "Rita Joe," in *A Woman's Almanac: Voices from Atlantic Canada*. Marian Frances White (ed.). St. John's, NF: Creative Publishers, 1995. pp. 41-3.

Smith, Gordon E., and Kevin Alstrup. "Words and Music by Rita Joe: Dialogic Ethnomusicology." *Canadian Folk Music Journal* 23 (1995). pp. 35-53.

Steele, Charlotte Musial. "Rita Joe Wages Gentle War of Words." *The Atlantic Advocate* (January, 1991). pp. 11-3.

Films/Videos:

Guns, Brian. *Song of Eskasoni: Reflections of Rita Joe*. Halifax, NS: Sunrise Films, 1993.

Nova Scotia Department of Education. *The Song Says It All*. Halifax, NS: Nova Scotia Department of Education, 1988.

Reeves, Darryl. *My Shadow Celebrates*. Halifax, NS: ATV, 1993.

Poetry Books by Rita Joe

Lnu and Indians We're Called, **Rita Joe.** In this, her third book of poetry, Rita Joe chronicles some of the important events in her life: her husband's death, her reunion with a brother after 20 years of separation, her life in foster homes and her nomination for the Order of Canada in 1990. These spiritual poems speak simply and powerfully to all readers.

"Rita Joe exemplifies the artistic assertiveness and cultural pride of the Mi'kmaq." *Daily News*

ISBN 0-921556-22-5 $9.95

Song of Eskasoni: More Poems by Rita Joe, **Rita Joe.** These eloquent poems cover a variety of themes: the ancient history of Rita Joe's people, the land they traditionally have inhabited and the struggles of Aboriginal people to recover their dignity despite racism.

"Not often enough can we enjoy such a wise and rich book of poetry." *Books in Canada*

ISBN 0-920304-85-0 $9.95

Ragweed Press titles are available at quality bookstores. Ask for our titles at your favourite local bookstore. Individual, prepaid orders may be sent to: **Ragweed Press**, P.O. Box 2023, Charlottetown, Prince Edward Island, Canada, C1A 7N7. Please add postage and handling ($3 for the first book and 75 cents for each additional book) to your order. Canadian residents add 7% GST to the total amount. GST registration number R104383120. Prices are subject to change without notice.